# A WRITER'S PARIS

a guided journey for the creative soul

**WRITER'S DIGEST BOOKS**
Cincinnati, Ohio
www.writersdigest.com

# A Writer's Paris

a guided journey for the creative soul

ERIC MAISEL

*with illustrations by*
*Danny Gregory and Claudine Hellmuth*

**Illustrations by Danny Gregory** appear on pages iii, 3, 6, 12, 14-16, 22, 27, 36, 40, 43, 45-46, 49, 59, 68, 72-75, 80, 87, 89, 92, 98-101, 104, 111, 115, 119, 122, 129, 132-135, 139, 145, 147-148, 150, 159, 162, 169, 172, 181, 184, 189, and 193.

**Collages by Claudine Hellmuth** appear on pages v, x, 9, 20, 28, 33, 46, 54-55, 63, 73, 79, 95, 99, 108, 124, 140, 147, 154, 160, 165, 175, 190, and 211.

Visit our Web site at www.writersdigest.com for information on more resources for writers.

To receive a free weekly e-mail newsletter delivering tips and updates about writing and about Writer's Digest products, register directly at our Web site at http://newsletters.fwpublications.com.

09  08  07  06  05      5  4  3  2  1

Distributed in Canada by Fraser Direct, 100 Armstrong Avenue, Georgetown, ON, Canada L7G 5S4, Tel: (905) 877-4411. Distributed in the U.K. and Europe by David & Charles, Brunel House, Newton Abbot, Devon, TQ12 4PU, England, Tel: (+44) 1626 323200, Fax: (+44) 1626 323319, Email: mail@davidandcharles.co.uk. Distributed in Australia by Capricorn Link, P.O. Box 704, S. Windsor NSW, 2756 Australia, Tel: (02) 4577-3555.

Library of Congress Cataloging-in-Publication Data
Maisel, Eric.
  A writer's Paris : a guided journey for the creative soul / by Eric Maisel.
    p. cm.
  ISBN 1-58297-359-8 (flexibind : alk. paper)

1. Paris (France)—Intellectual life. 2. Paris (France)—Social life and customs. 3. Paris (France)—Description and travel. 4. Paris (France)—Guidebooks. 5. Creative writing. I.Title.

  DC715.M32 2005                                    2005010525

  914.4'3610484—dc22

Edited by Jane Friedman
Design by Grace Ring
Cover design by Grace Ring
Production coordinated by Robin Richie

F+W PUBLICATIONS, INC.

*for my Paris traveling companions Ann, Natalya, and Kira*

# Table of Contents

Introduction: A Degree in Paris . . . . . . . . . . . . . . . . . .1

01| A Day in the Place des Vosges
Support your artistic nature every day . . . . . . .5

02| Pure Flâneur
Practice flânerie, the art of strolling . . . . . . . .9

03| Apricots
You must take the bad with the good . . . . . . .17

04| The Musée d'Orsay When It Opens
To be the artist is to be the exception . . . . . .22

05| On Not Speaking French
You'll always find reasons not to write . . . . .26

06| Writing in Public Places
Exercise your craft in parks, subways,
and churches . . . . . . . . . . . . . . . . . . . . . . . .34

07| Hemingway Slept Here
Be less tourist and more artist . . . . . . . . . . .41

08| Your Novel in Six Months' Time
Plan for it and mean it . . . . . . . . . . . . . . . . .47

09| Privilege and the Place Vendôme
Envision writing as good for humanity,
not an unearned privilege . . . . . . . . . . . . . . .53

10| Human Scale
Paris teaches intimacy . . . . . . . . . . . . . . . . .58

## 11| Sartre and Inauthenticity
How to write authentically . . . . . . . . . . . . . .62

## 12| Mimes and Literary Agents
Deal with and appreciate the absurd . . . . . . . .67

## 13| Three-Week Books
Write in one big gulp . . . . . . . . . . . . . . . . . .76

## 14| On Support
If it is in your power to help,
help. If someone is in a position
to help you, ask . . . . . . . . . . . . . . . . . . . . . .80

## 15| The Pain of Perfect Little Parks
Beauty brings with it an odd prick of pain . . . .85

## 16| The Doable Dream
Some impossible dreams are not
even improbable . . . . . . . . . . . . . . . . . . . . . .91

## 17| The Professor of Nothing
The café is the writer's home . . . . . . . . . . . .102

## 18| Disrespecting Albert Camus
The nobility of the writer's occupation
is in resisting oppression and accepting
isolation . . . . . . . . . . . . . . . . . . . . . . . . . . .107

## 19| Gay Mayors
Celebrate the man responsible for
freeing the Parisian park grass . . . . . . . . . . .113

## 20| Rainy Day Lover
Don't blame someone else when
you aren't writing . . . . . . . . . . . . . . . . . . . .118

## 21| Eating an Elephant
Scratch the surface to produce dramas . . . . .122

## 22| An Idea for a Novel
Overcome your defensive,
chattering mind . . . . . . . . . . . . . . . . . . . .126

## 23| Smaller and Smaller
Make sacrifices for your art . . . . . . . . . . . .136

## 24| Picasso's Ghost
Meaning is primary; beauty is secondary . . . .143

## 25| Not Writing
Only one in a hundred writers will
ever write when visiting Paris . . . . . . . . . . .149

## 26| Second Chances
Make a heroic decision to persevere . . . . . . .157

## 27| The Great Escape
Whether or not people support you,
your dreams are your dreams . . . . . . . . . . .161

## 28| Motivated by Croissants
Engage your senses. Engage your
readers' senses . . . . . . . . . . . . . . . . . . . .167

## 29| Running Off
Explore other cities once you're in Paris,
but don't run away from your writing . . . . . . .171

## 30| With Your Daughter on the Rue de Rivoli
Visiting Paris as a lone wolf is not
the only option . . . . . . . . . . . . . . . . . . . . .175

## 31| Maya and Lemonade
Meaningfulness slides into meaninglessness unless you can convince yourself
that your journey matters . . . . . . . . . . . . . .179

## 32| If Not Paris, If Not a Year
Schedule regular writing retreats,
even if not in Paris . . . . . . . . . . . . . . . . . .183

## 33| Fearing Paris
In order to create, we must forget our
past failures . . . . . . . . . . . . . . . . . . . . . . .187

## 34| Au Revoir to the Place des Vosges
If you go to Paris, write.
When you get home, keep
writing . . . . . . . . . . . . . . . . . . . . . . . . . . .191

## A1| Appendix: A Planning Checklist . . . . . . . . . . . . . . .195

## A2| Appendix: Where to Write or Read . . . . . . . . . . . . .201

## A3| Appendix: Resources for Planning Your Trip . . . . . . . .211

# Introduction: A Degree in Paris | **00**

One of the main challenges you face as a writer is writing regularly. Willing yourself to go to Paris—to write—is one way to meet this challenge. Just willing yourself to go isn't enough—that would be a trip, an adventure, a vacation, but not what I have in mind. Going for the express purpose of writing and then writing when you get there are the kind of brave acts that can help turn your writing life around. This is less about what Paris will do for your heart and your mind and more about what taking such a step means. To travel to Paris for two weeks or six months *and to actually write during that time* is to change your relationship to your writing. It is to put your writing first.

In this sense, a degree in Paris is more important than a degree in creative writing. Paris is a physical place defined by its beauty and its openness to strolling. It is home to the entire intellectual history of the West, the place where modern art, modern writing, and modern philosophy were born. Paris is a place where artists gather, where a Czech filmmaker, a Russian choreographer, an African painter, and a poet from Providence are most likely to collide. Paris is a place of associations: It moves the mind, stirs the heart, and resonates forever. More importantly, Paris is the place you go when you mean to put your creative life first.

Paris has served as muse to generations of artists, even to those who have never visited her. How has she accomplished this feat? Countless artists and writers have tried to say. Paris feeds an artist, motivates her, galvanizes her, and makes her murmur, "This is my home." A mere glimpse of a photo of a Parisian street causes us to feel both uplifted and bereft, thrilled by what Paris implies and saddened not to be living there right now. We do not have to list the reasons for its allure to get to the bottom line: Paris is *the* place to write. Since it is the perfect place to write, it is the perfect place to commit to writing.

Of course, your main task is to write where you are, in whatever physical and psychological circum-stances you find yourself. Toward that end you must educate yourself not only about the mechanics of writing, but about what it takes to get to the computer every day. That's the education that matters. What might it mean to your creative life if you included, as part of your education as a writer, a risky experience like running off to Paris to write? Something on that order may be needed to unlock the trunk and let out

those thousand poems, those hundred short stories, that full shelf of novels or narrative nonfiction. Paris—or rather, your commitment to being a writer in Paris—may prove the key.

I hope that you will go to Paris and write. I want to tell you about what writing in Paris has been like for me, what ideas Paris has provoked, and what associations it has evoked. Spending a few weeks or a few months in Paris has never been easier. As Brad Spurgeon explained in the *International Herald Tribune*, "Little remains of expat café life as cheap travel and electronic communications have virtually wiped out the expatriate ethos. Paradoxically, those same developments make life more practical for writers who seek to escape from the conventions and restrictions of their home countries."

It is easy to find a Parisian studio for a month, and I'll tell you how. It's easy to keep up with your e-mail, to stay in touch with agents and editors, to find what you need, and to live cheaply and well. I am not asking that you throw over your life in order to experience Paris. This is not a book about expat living. I am only asking that you use Paris not as a tourist destination, but as a place to write, and that you make Paris one of the stopping points on your creative journey. It is that creative journey that I am really talking about.

# A Day in the Place des Vosges | 01

Each time I arrive in Paris I head directly for the Place des Vosges, the most beautiful square in the world. How many writers and painters have stumbled upon this famous Marais square and said, "Oh, I see. This is why I came to Paris!"? Once discovered, it becomes a place to be remembered. A working artist can spend whole days there—writing, soaking up the ancient and the contemporary, and living ideally. Surrounded by Renaissance townhouses whose street-level arcades are filled with cafés, art galleries, and (in summer) classical musicians, it is lively, quiet, shady, safe, inviting, and gorgeous. You can write for an hour, move to a café table under the arcade for an espresso, write some more, stroll twice around the square, and resume your writing.

During the morning hours, the Place des Vosges is cool, still, and mostly empty. Mothers and their children arrive at about ten. They head for the sandbox on the western side of the park, which is warmer in the morning than the identical sandbox on the eastern side. At about the same time, the first busload of tourists arrives, the passengers feeling self-conscious at such an early hour in so empty a place. Their guides fill the square with historical information in

**Place des Vosges**
This is the oldest square in Paris, with a ground floor arcade of 39 houses. It is a true square (140m x 140m) and is considered a prototype of residential squares later built in Europe.

French, Italian, German, and Portuguese—about Victor Hugo, who lived at No. 6, about Mozart, who played a concert here at the age of seven.

As noon approaches, the park begins to fill up. Workmen renovating nearby buildings come to eat their sandwiches. Men and women on the move stop for a moment to use their cell phones. Tourists who have been rushing through the Marais drop onto

benches. Lovers arrive. Wine bottles are opened to complete picnic meals. Books are read, set aside, picked up again. The afternoon passes with people coming and going, life flowing, and artists working. In the early evening, well-dressed couples stroll slowly around the square, waiting on their dinner reservations, as incongruous-looking as their eighteenth-century aristocratic counterparts.

A Writer's Paris

Tourists take their last pictures in the fading light. Worn-out backpackers nap on the grass. Two lovers sleep in one another's arms. A man who might be Monet pores over a street map. Children chase the red-legged pigeons. A last tour group arrives to be drilled with history. The facades of the buildings on the eastern side blaze red. The summer light fades; but there is still plenty left for writing.

What is the magic of this place? The wrought iron lamps are certainly beautiful, as are the low wrought iron fences shaped like bent twigs. The placement of the fountains is right, the arcades that surround the square are right, the red brick mansions are right—it is *all* right, but I don't believe the square's allure is only about golden proportions. It is the ethic, the cultural imperative. Here you are encouraged to sit and write and people-watch, to adjourn to a neighboring café and write and people-watch some more, to pass an entire day this way. This is not encouragement that you will receive in America.

You feel at home in Paris because the things that you care about—strolling, thinking, loving, creating—are built into the fabric of the city. Despite its negatives—eighteen million tourists annually,

A Day in the Place des Vosges

11 percent unemployment, large numbers of homeless people—Paris remains the place where you can feel comfortable decked out as a dreamy artist. The Place des Vosges supports your artistic nature. About how many places can that be said?

It is almost nine. A uniformed guard begins shouting and gesticulating. He is closing the Place des Vosges. Too bad. I will be forced to stroll the back streets of the Marais and stop for a glass of wine at a café. I pack up my pad and my pen. The guard is get-ting animated. We are not leaving quickly enough. Of course not, as he is unceremoniously rousing us from a beautiful dream.

A Writer's Paris

# Pure Flâneur | **02**

Paris is a physically small city comprised of twenty
arrondissements laid out like a pinwheel. The inner
arrondissements contain tourist attractions like the
Louvre, Notre Dame, the d'Orsay, and the Eiffel
Tower, while the outer arrondissements
include such features as the Bois de
Boulogne to the west, the Bois de
Vincennes to the east, Montmartre to the
north, and the Parc Montsouris to the
south. Most tourists skip the outer
arrondissements and experience Paris as a
very tidy, handy place. But even if you venture further afield, you can get anywhere
by métro in no time at all.

Carved out of France with a round
cookie cutter, contained by its peripheral
road, Paris is intentionally made to feel
small so that its citizens can enjoy it. It is a
protected zone, with the tenements that
house new immigrants rising beyond the city
limits, making Parisian schools better than
their suburban counterparts. This reversal
takes an American a few seconds to process.
Because of planned city management, even the poor-

est Parisian neighborhoods feel eminently more livable than the poor parts of American cities.

I walked every Paris arrondissement and never felt unsafe. Statistics indicate that there is as much crime (and even as much violent crime) in Paris as in any American city. It doesn't feel that way. This feeling of safety, which may reflect reality or may amount to some romantic mirage, is an important part of why you feel like strolling in Paris, not like scurrying along as if late for an appointment. You feel secure sitting in a park, even if you're the only person there. You feel relaxed rather than vigilant as you amble. Perhaps you shouldn't feel this safe; but you do.

Hence my recommendation: Stroll everywhere. This strolling is an integral part of your time in Paris. You can only write so many hours a day—even for the most productive, published authors, three or four hours of writing is often the maximum. The rest of the day is yours, which makes the devil's ears perk right up. If you like, you can shop, socialize, catch up on your Proust, or jog in the Bois de Vincennes. But a superb alternative to succumbing to the dangers of having time on your hands is the practice of flânerie, the French invention of strolling as art form.

  A Writer's Paris

The flâneur is an observer who wanders the streets of a great city on a mission to notice with childlike enjoyment the smallest events and the obscurest sights he encounters. Baudelaire, a resident nineteenth-century flâneur, observed, "For the flâneur it's an immense pleasure to take up residence in multiplicity, in whatever is seething, moving, evanescent and infinite. You're not at home but you feel at home everywhere; you see everyone, you're at the center of everything, yet you remain hidden from everybody." This is one astute definition of the writer: an observer who ventures everywhere while remaining invisible.

You can stroll in New York but the Tao of New York demands double time. You can stroll in Los Angeles but the Zen of Los Angeles requires four wheels. You can stroll in your small town, but you will run out of sights and strolling room in three minutes flat. Most places are not designed or equipped to support two or three hours of ambling. It is in Paris that the delicious, dreamy strolling of the flâneur can be perfected. Indeed, you may never become the poet of your dreams until you become a poet of flânerie. It is the exercise regimen of the artist.

In Paris virtually every district is beautiful, alluring and full of unsuspected delights, especially those that fan out around the Seine in the first through the eighth arrondisements. This is the classic Paris, defined by the Arc de Triomphe and the Eiffel Tower to the west and the Bastille and the Panthéon to the east. Everything within this magic parallelogram is worth visiting on foot. … From St-Germain I like to work my way down the rue Bonaparte past the furniture and fabric stores, the Académie des Beaux Arts and the shops selling prints, finishing at the Institute, the building that houses the French Academy and its library, the Bibliotheque Mazarine.
  —from *The Flâneur* by Edmund White

The Pulitzer Prize-winning journalist Stanley
Karnow arrived in Paris in the early 1950s. He
recalls "whipping through Notre-Dame, the Sainte-
Chapelle, the Tuileries, the Palais Royal, the Place
de la Concorde, the Champs-Elysées, the Arc de
Triomphe" and all the other mandatory tourist sights.
Then he saw the light. "Presently, realizing that I
could not appreciate Paris unless I curbed my frenetic
pace, I became a flâneur—an aimless stroller in a town
ideal for aimless strolling. I would wander along the
Seine, pausing to browse for old prints in the quay-
side bookstalls, or watch the barges as they cruised up
and down the river, their decks festooned with laun-

dry, their sterns flying French, Dutch, British, and other European flags."

Flânerie fills up idle time beautifully and promotes that meditative state that leads to artistry. Vary your strolling by taking the métro each day to a new neighborhood, even inauspiciously bourgeois ones like the 15th or the 16th arrondissements, and begin your wandering. Stroll, stop for a snack, venture into a museum like the Air and Space Museum (Musée de l'Air et de l'Espace), the Buddhist museum (Musée National des Arts Asiatiques), or the Baccarat crystal museum (Musée Baccarat), smile, and pause to write. Wander on. Punctuate your stroll with cafés and churches. At the end of such a day you will sleep very well.

Even if your hometown isn't an auspicious place to practice flânerie, practice it anyway. This will hone your observation skills, model the writing life for young poets peeking out from behind their curtains as you pass, and prepare you for Paris. It will get you sunlight and exercise and put a smile on your face. Best of all, it will spark your writing. The walking meditation known as flânerie is a key that unlocks your creativity.

## Gargoyles in Paris

During one visit to Paris, I find myself tasked by a friend with locating a gargoyle suitable for petting. As everyone knows, there is no shortage of gargoyles in Paris. Notre Dame alone has tons of them. But those gargoyles are where they're supposed to be—high up and out of reach, where they can best perform their function as waterspouts. Finding a gargoyle at petting level is no easy task.

As I go out each day to write, I keep my eyes peeled. After a few days, I begin to see gargoyle mirages—mirages that turn out to be passers-by scowling. If I spoke French, I might ask around (and indeed it would be appealing to inquire of a shopkeeper or a gendarme, "Monsieur, where might I go to pet a gargoyle?"). But I haven't the French for such a sentence and must rely upon happy accident.

One morning, having just about given up on finding a suitable gargoyle, I stroll over to a small park on the Left Bank just opposite Notre Dame. After writing, I poke about the bins in front of Shakespeare & Company, almost buying but finally passing on various cheap editions of the Romantic poets. I proceed to wander through the warren of alleys where my favorite Greek sandwiches live. Choosing among the hawkers, I buy a sandwich piled high with fries, and amble away from the Seine, looking for a good spot to eat and make a mess.

I spot a friendly park and spend the next hour eating and addressing the question of the day: Are all obsessions dangerous, even the good ones; and, if they are, is it possible that the rewards can still outweigh the risks? Life can't get much better than a sunny day, a messy sandwich, and a worthy question. I vanish, as writers do. Cathedral bells chime as I make notes for a book with the working title of *Beethoven's Brain*.

After I conclude lunch, I turn a corner and come upon a building's entrance. I have happened upon the Musée de Cluny, Paris's storehouse of things medieval. My heart begins beating a little faster. Where better to find a stray gargoyle? I pass through an arch and enter a courtyard. There it is!

In the courtyard sits an old well, and sticking straight out at chest level from the well surround is a gargoyle perfect for petting. I am too excited to notice whether it is defecating or picking its nose or doing anything outrageous (as most gargoyles are). I rush back to my studio to report, and learn later that this gargoyle has far exceeded the expectations of the person at whose behest I have been looking. She informs me that it is so right a gargoyle that she has devoted a whole clip of photos to memorializing it.

Read up on gargoyles. They are very Parisian, very medieval, and have lots to say about what you'd be up against if you were a French peasant circa 1600 with aspirations in the arts or sciences. High above you, defecating and dripping snot, a host of spouting gargoyles would be watching your every move.

# Apricots

One summer morning I go out shopping for fruit at
the open-air market on the Boulevard Richard-
Lenoir. The prices at the multiblock market are low—
whole pineapples at the equivalent of 75¢ each,
apricots at 40¢ a pound—and, after curbing my
enthusiasm to buy everything, I decide on the apricots. As I approach one of the fruit-and-vegetable
stalls, I notice a woman selecting individual apricots
and putting them in a paper bag. I do the same,
selecting the good ones and avoiding the bad ones.

A young Arab minding the long row of produce
hurries over to us, lectures the woman, hands her the
scoop that has gotten buried among the apricots, and
orders her to scoop. I don't know what the two of
them are saying, but it's perfectly clear what he
intends to communicate. *At these prices*, he is telling
her, *you don't get to pick just the good ones. You take the bad with
the good. That's the deal.*

The woman doesn't agree. She makes a *Go away,
don't bother me!* gesture, utters some choice words of her
own, and keeps selecting the good fruit. He chides her
some more and, confronted by her stony indifference, throws up his hands. Then he turns to me. I
scoop. But it isn't simply to avoid a scene. The idea

**Richard-Lenoir Market**
This market, near the
Bastille, is open on
Thursday and Sunday
mornings. You'll find stall
after stall of fresh foods.

appeals to me tremendously, as it is an antidote to the
more usual idea that the good should arrive without
flaws and blemishes.

Taking the bad with the good is a principle that writers need to learn. The victims of endless advertising, we
have been brainwashed into fully misunderstanding
basic ideas like good and bad. As one example of this
malady, we are taught to expect *only the best*. What does *only
the best* mean? It means that we feel we are entitled to
something like perfection in our goods and services, that
it is unseemly to talk about the failures and mistakes that
were part of the process, and that things get our stamp of
approval based almost entirely on how they appear.

In a modern supermarket, everything looks perfect. Nothing is ever ripe, but the displays look so
good. In a modern movie, the production values are
beyond belief. The movie may be silly and beneath
contempt, but it certainly *looks* splendid. Where and
when are we taught to take the bad with the good? We
aren't! Instead we are bombarded with the opposite
message: *This is shiny! This is new! This is hot! This is perfect! This
is good! And nothing bad happened along the way!*

In order to create, you must take the bad with the
good. You are bound to write many bad paragraphs

along with the good ones. That is the eternal law. You can get rid of those bad paragraphs later, but first you must write them. Otherwise you won't write anything. If you try to write only the good paragraphs, you will paralyze yourself. You will fall victim to perfectionism, even if you aren't consciously trying to be perfect. Understand that the good *requires* the bad, that getting to the good is a process that includes mistakes and messes.

It doesn't seem to matter how many well-respected authors confess to needing twelve drafts to get their novels right, or three years of false starts to get their stage plays on solid footing. Even when a Nobel Prize winner announces that his first three novels stank, still the millions of would-be writers listening to these remarks do not hear what's being said. They do not hear that a writer can't avoid the bad, even if his life were to depend on it. They do not hear—that is, they deny—that they *must* take the bad with the good because the bad is part of the process.

If you want to understand the concept of denial, just visit with a writer not writing his novel because

"it isn't going well." Say to that writer, "Isn't the best plan to get a draft of your novel written—whether that draft is good, bad, or indifferent—and then see where you are?" Just watch his reaction. He will demonstrate one textbook example or another of psychological defense. His unstated fear is that a bad draft will mean that he is a bad writer, that he is a phony, that he has no chance. It doesn't. It never has meant these things and it never will. A bad draft does not possess that meaning at all. But he thinks it does.

Everything changes the instant you accept that you are bound to do lots of inferior work. Then no particular piece of inferior work is much of a blow. You just burn it and get on with your masterpiece. How wonderful can your writing be if you are tied to the idea that only gems must emerge from your pen? Imagining those gems is like imagining those perfect tomatoes piled high in a frigid supermarket, impervious to harm because of their genetically engineered leather skins. Don't let them impress you!

Paris is a golden opportunity to make messes. It is the perfect place to write the pitiful along with the wonderful, the short story from hell that becomes the short story from heaven, the screenplay with no plot that becomes the epitome of muscled narrative. Forget about masterpieces! Just come ready to write. Come with ideas, hope, and a genuine willingness to take the bad with the good. Take your cue from that bin of apricots, filled with rock-hard fruit, perfect beauties, and rotten leftovers. Just scoop! It's a real character builder.

# 04 | The Musée d'Orsay When It Opens

When you find yourself in Paris, you find yourself in the psychological, spiritual, and—in many cases— literal home of the painting revolution that occurred from the late nineteenth century through the early twentieth century. Seeing the art of this period in its home of Paris enriches the experience. Although you are in Paris to write, you will also sightsee; and one place you don't want to miss is the Musée d'Orsay.

The d'Orsay is a transformed train station that houses France's modern art collection. You must go there as an artist and not as a tourist, which means that you must go when you can actually commune with the art that hangs there. If you visit the d'Orsay at two in the afternoon, you will find yourself packed in like a sardine, one of a thousand other visitors. Elbowing your way from gallery to gallery, your only thought will be *Why am I doing this?* But if you visit the d'Orsay on a weekday morning when it first opens, you will have that great museum almost entirely to yourself for at least a full hour.

Arrive at the d'Orsay at 9:15, climb to the top where the Impressionist and Postimpressionist paintings hang, and enter a room full of Van Goghs. His paintings are beautiful and very different from their reproductions. *The Painter's Room at Arles* (*La Chambre de Van Gogh à Arles*) is brighter, more vivid than you expected. Suddenly his decision to paint garishly, out of a fear that his pigments would fade over time, makes perfect sense. As much as they have faded, his paintings are still bright and wonderful.

The Gauguins, too, are very moving. All at once you want to take his irony—those mocking words in his Tahitian journal that caused you to dismiss him as bitter and syphilitic—with a grain of salt. At 10:00 A.M. on a drizzly Thursday, in an underlit room with all these paintings surrounding you, you peer into Gauguin's heart and see that he was gentle. You ignore the fact that he ridiculed Van Gogh, and remind yourself that he also praised him. Gauguin is redeemed at this time of the morning in a way that he can't be redeemed later in the day, when hundreds of souls pack this small gallery.

**Gauguin and Van Gogh**
The two artists met in 1887 in Paris. Their friendship and correspondence sparked the creation of the Studio of the South in Arles, France. For two months they worked together in close quarters, with an intensity that Van Gogh described as "excessively electric." Before long, they had a falling out that led to the now-famous incident of Van Gogh cutting off his ear. The two artists never saw each other again after that.

At this early hour, all of the d'Orsay's amenities are yours. You can use the bathrooms without getting in line. You can shop in the museum store without getting shoved. In the gallery rooms you'll find comfortable rattan chairs, more humane and romantic than benches. If you happen to choose my preferred chair, you will have five Monets to enjoy, five views of the Rouen cathedral.

Downstairs, on the ground level, is an early Monet, painted when he was twenty-eight, as captivating as anything I've seen. It's a snow scene called *The Magpie (La Pie)*, painted the winter of 1868. On a snow-covered fence sits a single magpie. The magpie is one small black spot, and yet it balances all that snow. There is a secret here for the writer, a secret about the importance of every single word.

Finding yourself in such an eloquent church, how will you pray? By pulling out your pad and writing. We work in that silence that Kierkegaard called "the last scrap of Christianity left," the silence of book-store niches, shuttered studios, empty museums. The d'Orsay at ten in the morning is a writer's church, and our practice is to pull out our pads and write. No one can say who or what we're praising as we quietly scribble; but praise is surely in our hearts.

It makes all the difference in the world whether you visit the d'Orsay at 9:30 or at 3:00. Arriving at 9:30 is an act of devotion. Many writers come to Paris and then fall into step with the tourists. Be the exception and do the tourist sites in an artful way. Write wherever you find yourself, whether in a café or the Louvre, whether on a park bench or sitting in a blissfully empty gallery at the d'Orsay.

# 05 | On Not Speaking French

How might you talk yourself out of going to Paris? By tallying the cost; by picturing a cold, rainy January day on the Champs-Elysées; by arguing that if you aren't writing in your comfy apartment, you won't write in your cramped Parisian studio; by wondering how your cat and your lover will manage while you're away. Once you start on this list, it will run the length of your arm.

One way that you can talk yourself out of Paris is by reminding yourself that you don't speak French. Tell me, though—how much French do you think you will really need? You would need an awful lot to translate *Finnegans Wake* into French, to be sure, but almost none to order a cup of coffee, and *absolutely* none to write in English. You are not in Paris to study archaeology at the Sorbonne—you are not in Paris to *speak*, but to *write*.

For just about anything you need, you can simply point and say *Un comme ça* ("One of those"). This will work for a croissant, an umbrella, a roasted pigeon, an alarm clock, and probably for sex. Beyond that, you will need to know *Combien?* ("How much is that?"), numbers, and *Je suis désolée!* ("I am terribly, frightfully sorry!"). The phrases in your phrase book should get you on and off the right train and in and

out of the toilet. A small electronic French-English, English-French translator might come in handy, as might a good slang book. That's plenty!

If no emergencies arise during your stay and if you can manage your housing arrangements without a knowledge of French—which should be possible if the ads you answer are in English—you can glide through everything else virtually mute. You can spend an hour in the Monoprix (the French supermarket chain) familiarizing yourself with more yogurt possibilities than you ever dreamed possible, choosing between this or that chocolate mousse in the endless pudding section (they will all be delicious), and learning the art of bagging fruits and vegetables (you weigh them

**Monoprix** offers not only foodstuffs, but also brand-name personal hygiene products at great prices. You can find locations througout central Paris.

and price them yourself), without needing to utter a word. All you need to do is wheel your cart to the checkout counter, watch the register for the final tally, and pull out enough money.

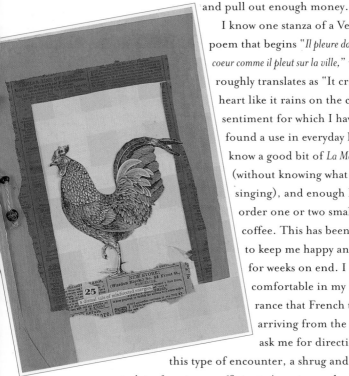

I know one stanza of a Verlaine poem that begins "*Il pleure dans mon coeur comme il pleut sur la ville,*" which roughly translates as "It cries in my heart like it rains on the city," a sentiment for which I have never found a use in everyday life. I also know a good bit of *La Marseillaise* (without knowing what I'm singing), and enough French to order one or two small cups of coffee. This has been enough to keep me happy and healthy for weeks on end. I look so comfortable in my igno-rance that French tourists arriving from the provinces ask me for directions. For this type of encounter, a shrug and a *Je ne parle pas français* are sufficient. Americans who know lots

of French often hate Paris and its citizens. I stand by my ignorance and ineptitude.

It is, however, real ineptitude. For a while I thought that you could live in Paris incredibly cheaply because I would see, among the ads for apartments in the windows of real estate offices, the occasional ad for a place a whole order of magnitude cheaper than the others. This excited me and may even have been the impetus for beginning this book. Then one day it dawned on me what those ads were advertising: They were ads for garage rentals. Did I feel like an idiot? Yes. Did I care? No.

To be sure, if you want a personal service, you may have trouble ordering it. You might get in a taxi and arrive not at the House of Fish (Maison des Poissons) but at a Museum of Poison (Musée de Poison). Writing out what you need—even if it's in garbled French—may help. Even better, and doable since you have time on your hands, is to wander around and hunt up English-speakers. My daughter Kira spent a week listening at the doors of beauty salons for the sounds of an English-speaking snipper. Finally she found one. Since she wanted only microns clipped from her hair, this was a crucial expenditure of time. She deemed her haircut a complete success.

**A Few French Slang Terms**

*Un navet*
Turnip, a derogatory term
for a new movie

*Une andouille*
Sausage, derogatory term
for a person

*Se frapper le biscuit*
Literally "to hit your
biscuit," to worry

I took several years of French in school, but they amounted to a complete waste of time. All that I remember about junior high school French class is that I took a fancy to fountain pens and spilled ink on my French reader. In high school, my French teacher substituted not-quite-off-color jokes for French instruction. (Question: What's the definition of a gentleman? Answer: Someone who doesn't pee in the shower.) In college I took French for one semester and flunked spectacularly. My F was so solid that you could have built a skyscraper on it. As if any of that could stop me from writing in Paris!

If you want to write in Berlin, do not let your lack of German stop you. If you want to write in Budapest, if you want to write in Seville, if you want to write in Rome—just do it. Take a language class first, if you must; get proficient, if that feels important; but remember that you are going off to write, not to chat. You might, as a test, keep track of how many crucial conversations you currently have with bus drivers, butchers, florists, and head waiters. That number probably approaches zero. Conversely, how often in life can you get by with "One of those, please"? Memorize *Un comme ça, s'il vous plaît* and start packing.

There are always reasons not to write. They appear as wantonly as toadstools after the rain. Entertaining those reasons even for a split second is the path to uncreativity. Write, even if you have a twinge, a doubt, a fear, a block, a noisy neighbor, a sick cat, thirteen unpublished stories, and a painful boil. Write, even if you aren't sure. Come to Paris, even if you don't speak French.

# Do French and Americans Get Along?

An American writer, a Francophile, tells me the following story.

She loves Paris and lives there whenever she can. She speaks French, though her command of the language is modest and her grasp of idioms imperfect. She's been staying in a room above a café, and the café owners are her landlords. She believes that they like her and they chat and laugh a lot together. She asks them to call her by her first name and she goes about introducing herself that way, believing that her last name is hard for the French to pronounce. So she says "Hello, I am Madame Irene" to the people she meets. Sometimes this gets her a funny look and a snicker, which she chooses to ignore.

One day a friend overhears her introducing herself this way. The friend gasps and pulls Irene aside. "You mustn't introduce yourself that way! In French, to use 'Madame' with your first name means that you run a brothel. You are introducing yourself as that kind of Madame!"

Irene thinks this is very funny. Still, she is a bit disturbed that her café friends have let her go on like this—have let her, well, make a fool of herself. She makes a point of mentioning it when she returns in the afternoon.

"Why didn't you tell me?" she asks, chiding them gently.

"Because we liked it!" they reply. "We thought it was funny!"

She is inclined to say that they were laughing with her. I am inclined to think that they were laughing at her. I would bet you a nickel that they were patronizing her, laughing at her romantic love of their city and their culture. That, at any rate, is my interpretation.

What's yours?

# 06 | Writing in Public Places

Writing in Paris is likely to entail writing in public—your hotel room or studio will likely be cramped, and you may find it hard to spend many consecutive hours in it. Because you are probably unaccustomed to writing in public, you may want to practice at home first. I've been writing in public for forty years and I love it. I especially love writing in bus stations. I've written in Mexican bus stations, Korean bus stations, Portuguese bus stations, Hungarian bus stations—all with equal pleasure.

In Paris I like to write at the Gallieni bus station. Connected to the last métro stop on the Gallieni line is a complex of restaurants and shops and, up some escalators and down some corridors, Paris's international bus terminal. In an immigrant neighborhood east of Paris, just over the border of the city, it is exactly where you'd expect a third-class transportation option to be located. Whether Canadian students, Arab migrant workers, or returning Romanians and Bulgarians, people taking the bus to Bucharest or Sofia expect no better.

Every few minutes a drama unfolds. One day I choose a bench in the boarding area for the Paris-London bus because the dramas there may unfold in English. Almost as soon as I'm seated, a drama commences. The British bus driver checking passports rejects a Chinese man and his wife. The driver gruffly explains that the man's passport is unacceptable. It contains contradictory information, indicating in one place that the man has a child and in another place that he doesn't. The Chinese couple will not be allowed on the bus. Suddenly they have no way to get from Paris to London and their flight home to China.

My imagination ignites. What if they have a child (the child alluded to in the passport), and he is currently staying with relatives in London? I spin out that novel, as any novelist would. It is a novel that begs to be written from the child's point of view. He is staying with relatives he has never met before. His parents, who have gone off on a small trip to Paris, fail to return. He wakes up one morning, it is drizzling in that London way....

No! I rein in my imagination and return to the nonfiction book I've come to work on.

Nearby the bus for Sofia is loading. A family seems to have lost something important, a piece of luggage,

a grandfather, a child. The bus driver is arguing in Bulgarian with two men who look like assassins. It seems that they don't have tickets but still expect to ride. The wild energy of loading commences; the lost family member, a young man, languidly appears; the passengers crowding around the bus pour aboard as if dropped down a funnel. At the last second the two assassins are let on.

A spy novel that would be fascinating to write suddenly invades me. No! I slap that novel away and return to my nonfiction. What a pleasant way to spend a few hours! You write what you intend to write and at the same time fill up your cup with a dozen new ideas

The real voyage of discovery consists not in seeking new landscapes, but in having new eyes.
—Marcel Proust

for books—books that you may never write, but that thrilled you for a few minutes.

On the way back, four young Brits board my métro car. At the next stop, two of the many gypsy musicians who ply the métro hop on. The Brits smile in recognition. The gypsies launch into a lively accordion-and-fiddle rendition of a folk tune that I've heard on the métro many times already. Then the strangest thing happens. The Brits, who must be conservatory students, start playing along with the gypsies in thin air.

One Brit plays the piano, the second plays the violin, the third the flute, the fourth the clarinet. They play perfectly. You can just tell. They keep tempo, dip when the music dips, bounce when the music bounces. They are completely serious (though mock-serious), four Cheshire cats performing their senior recital—knowing, physical, adroit, accomplished. It is a perfect Monty Python skit.

Next to me sit an African woman and her young daughter, a girl of six or seven. The girl has to peer around her seat to watch the musicians and the accompanying Brits, which she does with wide-eyed wonder. When we say that a child is born innocent, it is this look that we have in mind. It is entirely possible

that this girl will become a musician because of this moment; or a writer, penning a novel about a gypsy girl and a West End piano prodigy; or a painter who marries the smoky haze of jazz clubs with the heat of the African sun. Just look at her!

I hadn't planned to write, but how can I not? Leonardo said, "Always carry your little pad." What does it mean if you don't? What does it signify if you leave your writing tools at home? It takes no Freudian analyst to make the interpretation that you find it too easy not to write. Write in your company cafeteria, on the subway to work, in line at the home supply store. When a sight tugs at your heart, pull out your pad and write.

A Writer's Paris

## Writing in Churches

I often write in churches, more so in Paris than anywhere else. I love the ancient ones the best, the bare, vaulted ones, the simple stone ones that let in almost no light. Because it rains in Paris much of the winter and because, to keep to your austere writing regimen, you will need plenty of free places to write, you too will probably end up writing in churches. You may find yourself doing so even if your religion is writing rather than one of the traditional creeds.

Indeed, you may want to elevate your passion for writing to the level of faith. Here is a reasonable writer's creed. "I belong to the First Church of Writing. I affirm that truth, beauty, and goodness are cornerstone virtues of the human experiment, that individuals for whom this idea resonates must lead the way for others, and that writing is just another name for this reluctant leadership. I make some things up, I tell some useful truths, I try to use words wisely and well, and I make my meaning with a pad and pen."

We can't say with any precision what we worship, as it isn't creativity, human nature, soul, spirit, love, or life. What it's closest to may be the following: we worship our own moral nature and the heroic effort required of us to be true, beautiful, and good. We worship something in us that is the best the universe has to offer. Only potential until we free it, it is as real as iron once we act.

But living it!—there's the rub. If your daily routine is to wake up at dawn, take a quick shower, dive into rush hour traffic, make phone calls as you drive to work, and race headlong from task to task for the next fourteen hours, how does writing fit into your life? If you had a manor, gardens, servants, and an independent income, then perhaps you could write properly. But with life as you find it, where can you find the opportunity?

In Paris. That week, month or year that you carve out of a secular life to come to Paris is your time to write—and worship. Wander into Saint Julien le Pauvre, a Left Bank church dating back to around 1200. University meetings were held there until 1524, when student protests caused the parliament to ban all Sorbonne riffraff from the church. Now a Greek Orthodox church, Saint Julien is a perfect place to get out of the rain, contemplate your natural religion, and write. Use the churches of Paris for your own purposes. Who could begrudge you praying in your own way?

# Hemingway Slept Here | **07**

In Paris, every old stone, every leafy vista, every glimpse of the Seine evokes a nostalgic reaction, some combination of love and ennui. Paris can make us think of George Sand, Gertrude Stein, or F. Scott Fitzgerald, and not our novel-in-progress. This romantic reaction is right and proper but a trap, the trap of Paris as soulful museum, a place of anecdotes and literary attractions. If you are inclined not to write, or not quite sure what to write about, or just a little short of wherewithal, you will come to Paris looking for a Hemingway fix rather than an encounter with your own notepad.

I don't care where Hemingway slept. I'm not drawn to locate the exact spot in the Luxembourg Gardens where he pilfered pigeons for dinner. What writers write interests me. I'm also interested in their lives, in the exact nature of their heroism and foibles, in the stands they take, in their failures of nerve. What does not interest me, however, is that Joe Celebrity Writer lived in this studio or that a certain underappreciated poet frequented that café. How much more resonant is a cup of coffee at Les Deux Magots or Le Procope than the same cup at a charming café in your part of Paris? At Le

Procope the ghosts of dead poets and postmodernists add nothing except 100 percent to the bill.

I'm interested in the French physician and novelist Louis Ferdinand-Céline, who returned to his Parisian practice of medicine after a stint in Germany as a Nazi collaborator. He surrounded his home with barbed wire, posted guard dogs, and lacerated the Chinese instead of the Jews in his novels—the Jews posing less of a threat after the Holocaust. Céline the phenomenon is fascinating. But I don't need to visit the spot where his guard dogs roamed.

There's nothing wrong with cultural tourism. I make my own pilgrimage to Monet's Giverny with my daughters, and we have a splendid day. But our happiness has nothing to do with Monet's house and gardens and everything to do with the ice cream cones we eat sitting on a stone step, and the way the day's sharp light will affect our future work. When you wake up in Paris each morning, let your first thought be *Where will I write?* and not *Whose ghost shall I stalk?*

If Hemingway is important, it is because what he had to say still touches us. But is it important that on this exact spot, now smack in the middle of a fancy mall, he had onion soup after a night of

debauchery? Hardly. The past is no substitute for the present. Love the 1440s, love the 1680s, love the 1920s—love any epoch that touches your soul. But start each day focused on your writing and not on your literary maps.

In her book *Found Meals of the Lost Generation: Recipes and Anecdotes From 1920s Paris*, Suzanne Rodriguez-Hunter describes her unsatisfying experience chasing literary ghosts. She explains: "Like many others with a literary bent and a passion for the expats, I often toured the Montparnasse hotspots of yesteryear. I dallied on the sidewalk before the ancient building where Ernest and Hadley Hemingway first lived in 1921, I stood outside 27, Rue de Fleurus, imagining

**27 Rue de Fleurus**
Gertrude Stein's home at 27 Rue de Fleurus became a popular salon that reached its peak in the 1920s. Some of her famous guests included Picasso, Hemingway, and Fitzgerald.

Gertrude Stein's studio hung floor to ceiling with the most explosive art of the century. This was all great fun, but something was missing. I was on the outside looking in. I resigned myself to this fact until one day I stumbled onto a way I could participate here and now with there and then."

Her participation was to research and write her book. It is only by participating—that is, by creating—that cultural tourism makes sense to the writer. You may go to a famous cafe; but you go to write. You may fill your head with anecdotes of the lost generation; but only if those anecdotes constitute grist for your mill. You may sleep in a room in which Hemingway slept, but so as to dream your own work. Adopt this orientation whenever you travel: less tourist, more artist.

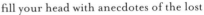

## The Intellectual Tradition of Paris

You can do one or another of an infinite number of tours of Paris, this one following the path of Jake Barnes through Hemingway's *The Sun Also Rises*, that one leading you to the ateliers of Picasso, Modigliani, and Chagall, a third guiding you around Napoleon's Paris. You could focus on sewers, on catacombs, on the evolution of the Marais from Jewish quarter to tourist mecca. Most poignantly and importantly, you can choose to engross yourself in the intellectual history of Western thought. Virtually any idea you can think of has been birthed or batted about in the studios, classrooms, and cafés of Paris—it is the birthplace of the humanistic tradition.

Sadly, the casual tourist is hammered into believing that the history of Paris has everything to do with Notre Dame's start date and completion date. Facts of that sort don't interest the tourist, but he feels obligated to listen, just as his tour guide feels obligated to tell bad jokes. The writer, painter, or composer who visits Paris should abandon this pointless bandwagon and instead read *The Social Contract* or *Candide*, Cora Sandel's *Alberta and Freedom* or Jean Rhys' *Night Out 1925*, Elsa Triolet's *Paris Dreaming* or Christina Stead's *The Beauties and the Furies*. Bask in ideas, not in statistics.

If I were Paris, I would rather you knew the myriad ideas I'd embraced over two plus millennia, not the number of objects I had stored up in the Louvre. While Paris is the perfect place to create, it is also the perfect place to engage in intellectual rather than traditional history. Skip learning which bridge was built when or which statue commemorates which noble prince. Instead, throw yourself into a week-long, month-long, or year-long exploration of some striking idea. It is splendid to do this in Paris; it is no less splendid to do this at home.

# Your Novel in Six Months' Time | **08**

Imagine that you've managed financially and emotionally to set yourself up with a six-month writing jaunt in Paris. Congratulations! Here is a perfect plan for those six months. It posits three writing stints a day: two hours in a park, two hours in a café, two hours in your tiny studio (or some similar routine). Yes, that *is* a lot of writing! But that's the point. You have come to Paris to write, not just to stroll and have adventures. The croissants and museums will take care of themselves. You must take care of the writing.

**Day 1.** Arrive in Paris. Gather your wits. Collapse.

**Day 2.** Look for your rental (if you haven't arranged one from home). Walk everywhere. Savor.

**Day 3.** Look for your rental. Walk everywhere. In a café, pull out the notes for your novel. If you haven't begun your novel yet, entertain ideas. Massage your feet when you get back to your room.

**Day 4.** Secure your rental for the first of the following month. Celebrate by writing. Splurge on a snack, perhaps a L'Opéra pastry and a really big cup of coffee. If you don't have an idea for a novel yet, ask for help from a passing American tourist. Say "Excuse me, I'm about to write a novel and need to choose among the following ideas. Which of these

What a heavy thing is a
pen!
—Émile Zola

novels would you most like to read?" Ignore your respondent's advice, but take careful note of your own reactions.

**Day 5.** Commence your writing routine of three writing stints a day. With luck, this will amount to six pages a day (two pages a stint). Six pages a day is a novel in two months' time. If you can manage it, you will be well ahead of schedule!

**Day 6.** Write.

**Day 7.** Write.

**Day 8.** Write. Visit the Red Wheelbarrow bookstore in the Marais, or some other anglophone bookstore. Practice your English. Swap writing-in-Paris stories. Make a date with a stranger for coffee. Say to the bookstore owner, "When my novel comes out two years from now, can I do a book-signing here?" That way you'll have your first book-signing arranged.

**Day 9.** Write. Have coffee with that stranger. Write or make love, or both.

**Day 10.** Write, unless you feel the need to read what you've written so far. Be careful! If you decide to read, be ready for a shock. You may have made a mess, and you may need to regroup. On the other hand, you may love what you've written. In that case, exult. Exult by writing.

**Day 11.** Take a day trip to Monet's house in Giverny. Write on the métro to the commuter train. Write on the train to the bus. Write on the bus to Giverny. (Don't miss your stop!) Write on a bench with a view of the Japanese footbridge. Wander over to the Museum of American Impressionism (Musée d'Art Américain) just down the road and use one of their excellent bathrooms. Write on the stone bench in front of the museum. (Don't miss the last bus! They stop running early in the day.) Write on the bus to the commuter train. Etc.

**Day 12.** Maybe the blues have stuck. Splurge on a mystery, maybe one set in a Paris arrondissement, and read it all the way through. Talk to someone. Fall in love. Don't worry about writing today. But plan to write tomorrow.

With each book you write, you should lose the admirers you gained with the previous one.

—André Gide

**Day 13.** Say *au revoir* to your lover. Back to work! Write, write, write.

**Day 14.** Two weeks in Paris! Catch up with your e-mail at an Internet cafe. Have a nice lunch followed by a two-scoop Berthillon ice cream cone. Nap by the Seine.

**Days 15-64.** Write, write, write.

**Day 65.** You are practically a native. You can get around, you can get your hair cut. How are your finances? Better check and see. How are your emotions? If you're feeling too weird, take a mental-health day. Remind yourself that writing in Paris is a brilliant way to make meaning and that you are absolutely on track. Make this sales pitch work. If necessary, treat yourself to chocolate. If you haven't been writing enough (or at all), release your guilt and embarrassment and start fresh. Consider it Day 1.

**Days 66-98.** Write, write, write.

**Day 99.** Three months is a long time! If you've been writing on a daily basis, you will have written thousands of words. Should you read and revise, or just keep writing? If it has been your habit to write without revising and that habit has gotten you into trouble before, bravely read what you've written. Weep for the parts that don't work and revel in the parts that do. If, on the other hand, it has been your habit to revise so tightly that you end up with constipated nuggets, skip revising. Keep writing. You can read what you've written when you get back to Boise.

**Days 100-134.** Write, write, write.

**Day 135.** You've spent more than four months living in Paris. Hardly one in a million writers pulls off this feat. Celebrate by buying a silly hat and taking a day trip to Chantilly or Fontainebleau, two forests-with-castles just outside of town. Picasso used to visit Fontainebleau to "gorge on green" (so he could then disgorge all that green when he got back to the studio). In the evening, buy a CD of Parisian café songs and play them at a friend's apartment.

**Days 135-168.** Write, write, write.

**Days 169-179.** Catch some of the sights you missed by writing so much: the Musée Rodin, the Paris sewers, Voltaire memorabilia at the Musée Carnavalet. Pat yourself on the back. Get ready for the long flight home.

**Day 180.** Say *au revoir* to Paris, but not good-bye. If you are braver than anyone I know, read your manuscript on the plane.

Giving birth to a book is always an abominable torture for me, because it cannot answer my imperious need for universality and totality.
—Émile Zola

If you pull off the heroic feat of writing in three stints a day, you will actually write your novel in six months' time. This is no pipe dream—it will absolutely happen. It could also happen right where you are. If you have a day job or similar commitments, follow this plan: one writing stint at five in the morning, one at lunch, and one in the evening. You will have a draft of your novel written in six months' time. I guarantee it.

# Privilege and the Place Vendôme | **09**

Maybe the following thought has popped into your head and is about to derail your plans for your Paris trip: *How arrogant of me to think of living the leisured life of a bohemian artist—even for just three months—when I could be helping the poor, mentoring middle school students, or getting on with a real profession and a real career.* I understand your concerns entirely. I'm a privilege-conscious person myself. Precisely these questions of privilege strike me as I cross the Place Vendôme one cloudy afternoon in July.

The Place Vendôme is a legendary place—the home of the Hôtel Ritz, its bars, and much Hemingway mythology. Here Hemingway drank. Here, legend has it, he welcomed the liberation of Paris by ordering seventy-three dry martinis for his new buddies, the first American troops to arrive in the city. You can still visit the Hemingway bar at the Ritz, though it's only used for special occasions nowadays. Does this mythology make the Place Vendôme feel romantic and literary? Not in the slightest.

The Place Vendôme has no benches, no trees, and no simple niceties. What it has are expensive shops and a towering statue of Napoleon. The occasional tour bus loads in the middle of the Place, so loitering is not strictly forbidden, but you sense that

someone is peeking out from Cartier to make sure that no rabble is gathering. The painter Gustave Courbet led exactly such a rabble against this bastion of privilege, toppling its central pillar during the heady days of the Commune. The intention was to replace Napoleon's statue with a monument to democracy and world unity. Courbet lost, and was forced to replace the original column at his own expense.

I hope that you will be able to come to Paris with enough money that you won't have to work at anything except your writing. If you can do this, however, you are in a privileged position—even if you labored for years to save for your adventure. Worse yet, maybe you didn't have to labor. Maybe you have affluent parents,

**Residents of the Place Vendôme** include (but are not limited to) the Hotel Ritz, Guerlain (perfumes), the sultan of Brunei, Buccelati (jeweler), Armani, Cartier, Bulgari, Chaumet (jeweler), Piaget, Chanel, Mauboussin (jeweler), Schiaparelli (designer), Van Cleef & Arpels, Charvet (designer), and Boucheron (jeweler).

A Writer's Paris

or married money. Won't that make your stay in Paris reek of privilege? How many Ethiopians or Peruvians can bop into Paris and write? If you can, you are among the world's royalty. Isn't that close to a sin?

No, it isn't. But if, emotionally and intellectually, you side with the world's downtrodden, and if you have enough money in your pocket for a sojourn in Paris, privilege may prove a real psychological impediment for you. First you will have to give yourself permission to come; then you will have to regularly reconvince yourself that writing on a park bench in a Paris square is a legitimate activity in a world of floods, famines, and the unequal distribution of wealth. I hope you can do that. If you criticize yourself for being indolent and indulgent, you are being reasonable in one sense but absurd

The more indignant I make the bourgeois, the happier I am.
—Gustave Flaubert

in another. Opt to see this absurdity. Consider writing in Paris to be good for humanity, and not an abuse of privilege.

And another worry: What if you convince yourself that going to Paris to write is absolutely legitimate, then go to Paris and don't write? There's a new pain! The fear that you may fail yourself and squander your time can combine with questions of privilege and make you doubt that you should make the trip at all. Demoralized by your vision of yourself as a privileged American stargazing and eating croissants, you may indict yourself for your aspirations and sentence yourself to house arrest back in Butte.

You should be praised for your conscience. It is good to know when you have something that others don't. It is righteous not to forget that people are suffering, and that part of your purpose is to help. That way of thinking is not neurotic self-flagellation (though it can become that), nor an excuse for not writing (though it can become that too). Your concerns are praiseworthy. Yet they are not reasons to forbid yourself the writing life. Generosity and compassion do begin at home. Not only must you grant yourself permission to go to Paris, but you

must picture yourself writing. Predict success; and if you can't predict success, at least don't predict defeat.

For a conscientious postmodern person, even the best impulses—like risking a year on a writing adventure—have moral ramifications. You might pass on Paris for practical reasons; you might pass for psychological reasons; you face one more potential obstacle as you ask yourself, *Is it decent and honorable to write in Paris when I could possibly be doing more good in some other way?* As to the answer to this particular moral question, I believe that right is on your side.

The Place Vendôme represents the negative aspects of privilege: privilege as a protected world, exclusionary and defensive, not wanting to be troubled by those it considers inferior. The privilege you are experiencing as a writer in Paris is something very different: It is the privilege of the lone individual fortunate enough and brave enough to follow her dream.

# 10 | Human Scale

Paris improves your writing because it teaches you something profound about intimacy. You can walk directly by the Seine—it is there for the touching. You can sit down at a café table and let life envelop you. You can enter an ancient church and use it as your study. These lessons infiltrate your writing and cause you to write more poignantly. You better understand gestures, epiphanies, and fleeting moments after your Paris education.

Consider the bridges of Paris. They are not five-mile-long traffic-clogged behemoths. They are short and sweet. You encounter one of these bridges and your first reaction is to stop. You want to prop your elbows up on the low stone wall, watch the boat traffic glide by on the Seine, and feel yourself transported. Your imagination is engaged, and some poem or short story starts growing. The scale of the bridge is such that dreams are invited and art flows.

Take the small bridge that connects the two Paris islands Ile de la Cité and Ile Saint Louis. The Pont Saint Louis epitomizes the genre of "intimate bridge." Everyone visiting Paris crosses this bridge and feels compelled to stop. You get a splendid (albeit rear) view of the Notre Dame cathedral a few hundred

feet away. You peer down at a slim finger of the Seine, so gentle that you want to baptize your child in it. Around you are Japanese chamber musicians playing a string quartet, or some Czech jugglers, or a French unicyclist, or a folksinger from Toronto looking (if not sounding) like Dylan.

Nearby are the sights that you've come to see. There is Notre Dame and the Hotel Rolland with its Moorish windows; lining the island's narrow streets are seventeenth-century great houses, now museums where you'll find Chopin, Sand, and Hugo memorabilia. Yet you feel in no rush to sightsee. Standing on

the bridge is more important. A bridge has existed at this spot for a thousand years—sometimes a footbridge, sometimes a traffic bridge. Once again closed to traffic, it is today at its most poignant.

This is the perfect place to test your skills as an unselfconscious writer. Sit right down on the sidewalk with your back nicely supported by the bridge wall. Pull your feet in (or stretch them out if you're feeling adventurous). Get out your pad and pen. Glance up once or twice to warm your forehead with a beam of sunlight, then bury yourself in your writing. It is hard to imagine a better place to start on your new novel or to find that missing word for your poem.

Thank you, Paris, for this lesson in scale. It is among the hardest lessons for a writer to learn. You want to show a war, but you must show a battle instead. You want to prove the greatness of a great love, but you can't do it through hyperbole—you can only do it by a careful noticing of the way your lovers hold hands. What writer doesn't prefer an intimate footbridge to the Golden Gate? Look around you in Paris and study her human-size things.

## Footbridges and Intimacy

One day I found myself on the Pont Saint Louis standing next to a thirty-year-old man and his sixty-year-old mother. He is reciting his grievances and she is listening with a silence at once tortured and stony. He worked; his father didn't. Why did she invariably side with his father? He was responsible; his father was irresponsible. Why did she love his father so much and him so little? More hurt than angry, he is ready to cry. Why did she never take his side? Why won't she admit the truth even today?

The setting has allowed him to speak. This conversation never could have occurred in their living room, at the supermarket, or at the Louvre. This bridge creates a place safe enough for a boy to speak to his mother. She refuses to reply, but Paris still has done him a great favor.

Not every bridge in Paris is worth eulogizing. Many are as ordinary as the ones back home—traffic-choked, a struggle to cross, functional, just steel and cement and a way to go. They do not invite pause and they hardly permit you to stop. But a few of Paris's bridges are exceptional. They are worth the airfare and the languid hours I pray you devote to them. They are why you came. Bring your pad; bring your pen; the rest is easy.

# 11 | Sartre and Inauthenticity

When we leave something out of a story, we lie—and we are always leaving something out. When we highlight something in a story, we lie—and we are always highlighting and underlining. It is therefore no paradox that writers are great liars and great truth-tellers. So be it!

While writers may lie incessantly, that is no justification for choosing to write insincerely. If we know that our argument is weak, it rests squarely on our shoulders to strengthen that argument or abandon it entirely. If we throw in a gratuitous scene to make fun of this or to rail aimlessly at that, we must edit out that scene when we revise. If we write in jargon so as to avoid saying what we mean or to disguise the fact that we haven't much to say, our own voice should shout, "No! Don't do that!" There is necessary lying; and there is old-fashioned, everyday lying.

Your time in Paris offers an opportunity to take your writing and your principles seriously. Gather up your integrity before you leave. Each of us can be clever, and if we only write cleverly, we've sacrificed that integrity. Each of us is capable of making fine distinctions, and if we only make fine distinctions we've acted indecently. We can create glittery edifices, pretty pictures, false idols—none of that will do. Our job is to write for humanity or against inhumanity. Then you can write with a microscope, focusing on a couple who live in close quarters in a cramped relationship, or with a telescope, about wars and the people who wage them.

Many writers pick up their pen with lesser agendas in mind. Take Jean-Paul Sartre, for instance. Sartre had it in mind to write for humanity, but his character failed him. He might have followed up a novel like *Nausea*, in which he made an honorable effort to wrestle with questions of meaning, with fiction or nonfiction that further articulated the meaning struggles of our species. He might have attempted the fine project he alluded to in an early essay, of constructing a coherent humanistic-atheistic

philosophy. Instead, to use the language of the existentialist, he never became, he dodged the encounter.

He dodged the Resistance. He assiduously skipped that hardest job of all, writing with his conscience engaged. There is no better example of this dodging and long-term bad faith than his absurd last effort, the many years he spent writing an unreadable biography of Flaubert. Years on a biography of Flaubert when you haven't articulated the principles of existentialism yet! That really won't do.

Essayist John Sturrock explained in *The Word From Paris*: "Sartre refused to give up writing his obsessive study of Flaubert, *The Family Idiot*, elitist in the extreme though he knew it to be, a barely accessible work of literary criticism that would never be read by more than a few people. It wasn't reasonable, he complained to interviewers, to expect him to abandon this huge piece of work, and he set to wondering, a little pathetically, whether one day, by some unspecified process of 'mediation,' 'this sort of book might serve the masses.' Which, for those who have attempted, and been worsted by, the outrageous size and frequent obscurity of the unmediated *Idiot*, has to rank as the most utopian of all of Sartre's speculations."

I hold Sartre accountable for his character and, in turn, his destiny. Like you and me, he could think, he could observe, he could intuit, he could analyze, he could synthesize. He just couldn't look in the mirror. This ubiquitous character flaw, the unwillingness to engage in self-awareness, is so commonly known and understood that we must suppose that Sartre knew about it. He might, if he'd been interested, have demanded of himself, "Am I guilty of inauthenticity for continuing my Flaubert biography?" I credit him with the power to ask such questions and, crediting him with that power, find him guilty.

The Greek philosophers and poets honored fate. They observed that people rarely changed and announced, "Character is destiny." The existentialist is not so ready to let man off the hook. We claim that man can look in the mirror and, if he is brave enough to stare, catch a glimpse of his own tricks. If you agree, then you also must agree that looking in the mirror is an integral part of your preparations for Paris. You have more than your pads and pencils to bring—you also have your courage and your conscience. Then, when you write in Paris, you will write authentically.

We do not do what we want, and yet we are responsible for what we are—that is the fact.
—Jean-Paul Sartre

Intend well. You may fail in the execution but if your intentions are honorable you'll be able to hold your head high. Is your intention to shed some light or to add to the darkness? Do you feel righteous or queasy when you begin a new piece? Do you respect your own writing motives? Ask these questions when, some sunny day in June, you sit in a Parisian café, your notebook open, and wonder, "What should I write next?" Do you want to spend a decade on a "biography of Flaubert for the masses"? Watch out!

A writer is the last person on earth permitted to ignore the distinction between authentic and inauthentic.

# Mimes and Literary Agents

I love mimes. There is something so absurd about their career choice that I have to smile. I love *all* of the absurd professions—for instance, new-genre public art, whose practitioners videotape ice melting, or make marks on rocks in the wilderness just to provoke the wind. I appreciate the wandering Zen poets who beg for food, Honoré de Balzac hiding behind the name Madame de Brugnol to dodge his creditors, and you and me, who dream of witnessing for the culture *and* making a living.

What, exactly, is a mime thinking? Well, for one thing, he must decide what sort of mime to be. Like the academic poet who thumbs his nose at the slam poet, the theater mime thumbs his nose at the street mime, decrying, as one theater mime did, "that illegitimate art whose practitioners bother pedestrians and demonstrate cliché illusions." So mimes are caught up in the same battles that you and I are about what constitutes art. Who knew?

Even in the absurd professions there are rivalries and heated debates. Doesn't that make you want to hug a mime? Paris is surely the place to do just that, as it is the spawning ground and training center of these absurd, friendly creatures. You can catch sight

**Marcel Marceau**

Born in 1923 in Strasbourg, France, Marcel Marceau is recognized as the world's greatest mime. He's toured the world 40 times, and New York City declared March 18 Marcel Marceau Day.

of the next Marcel Marceau or Jean-Louis Barrault trapped behind imaginary glass wherever tourists gather, especially in front of Notre Dame and the Centre Pompidou. And if you want to become a mime yourself, you can train right here at the École Internationale de Mimodrame de Paris Marcel Marceau.

Because their absurd choice of profession makes me smile, I pay the Parisian mimes their tribute. When I encounter one in red looking like a Victorian lampshade, a white-faced one looking more greasy than ethereal, or an energetic one on stilts dodging in and out among the tourists, I have to drop a euro into his or her collection plate. I must tithe at the mime's absurd church, which is also mine.

A Writer's Paris

Sometimes we exchange a glance—how delicious to receive a mime wink!

By contrast to the absurd professions, there is the profession (very important to you and me) of literary agent. One summer, while I am in Paris teaching at a conference, a literary agent appears and presents a two-part workshop on consecutive afternoons. Even though it is free to participants, the costs are very high. It isn't just the natural antipathy between art and commerce that gets inflamed by her presentation. It is the anger aroused by her cheerful dismissal of substance. We would like to hear a tiny bit about steak, but her lecture is about the art of sizzle.

She smiles as she ticks off her two main points: (1) pick a sexy topic and (2) hype it to the moon. She uses as her model of an ideal nonfiction book proposal a breathlessly hyped proposal for an Elvis Presley fanzine book that no one in the room would ever dream of writing. The agent gushes about the relentlessness with which the author has pitched his product. She does her best to convince us that a writer would be an idiot not to produce a proposal just as smart as this one.

When it comes time for questions, I try one out. "How would you hype an intelligent, small book that couldn't be expected to reach a large audience?"

"Don't say *small*!" she cries. "We never say *small*. We say *a book for a niche market*."

Indeed! I know that agents and editors talk about small books and big books all the time. I smile and keep smiling as she reiterates that anything can sell, just so long as you hype it and use phrases like *niche market*.

It is a harrowing afternoon and I do not come back the second day. I know this agent's message inside out and deliver part of it myself to the writers I coach. Publishing is a business. It is absurd but true that when your book on the museums of Paris or the natural history of Idaho comes out, it must compete not only with the twelve other books appearing that season from your own publisher, but with the thousands appearing from other publishers nationwide. It's as if every mime had to worry about eleven other mimes competing with him for attention. What a hubbub that would be! What a raucous silence!

It is also absurd but true that if we want to be published, we must listen to what publishers and marketplace players say. We have to sit still for a little lecturing and a little educating. At least, if this lecturing and educating occur in Paris, you can rush from the lecture hall and find a mime with whom to commiserate. Can't you just picture his smile turn into a frown as you tell him your sad story? Especially the part about twelve mimes gesticulating wildly for attention on every street corner?

## The Opinions of Others

 I have dinner with a French writer at an Algerian restaurant in the 20th arrondissement. He tells me that he has spent the afternoon assigning grades to his latest novel according to what the reviewers have said about it. In his estimation, of the ten reviews that have come out so far, two gave his novel an A, two gave his novel a B, two gave his novel a C, two gave his novel a D, and two gave his novel an F. He laughs and orders us another bottle of wine. I tell him the following story.

Several years ago I received word that I'd come in second in a prestigious national novel-writing competition. Coming in second in a national novel-writing competition is like coming in second in major league sports. You're a loser. Isn't that the way our culture thinks? Isn't that the way we ourselves think? Of course, we can reframe the matter and say *I came so far* or *I came this close*. We can say *What do they know?* or *Did I really enter that?* Still, when all is said and done, people who do not come in first feel like losers.

Actually I was busy with other things when the rejection letter arrived, and I didn't pay it much attention. After the first hundred rejections in a writer's life, each subsequent one is relatively easier to ignore—except for those that, for whatever reason, get under your skin. This wasn't one of the painful ones. The rejection letter was gentle and flattering and I really hadn't expected to win. I emptied the battered envelope (there is no envelope quite so battered-looking as one that returns a rejected manuscript) and prepared to put the manuscript away. As I went to put it away I noticed that someone had accidentally included two reader comments with the returned manuscript.

Here was a moment of truth. Did I dare read them? Did I want some "objective feedback"? Did I want some hurt feelings? I poured myself a whiskey and bravely (or foolishly) proceeded to take my medicine. One reader said, in an intelligent and carefully crafted paragraph, that the novel I'd submitted was among the best things he had ever read. The other reader said, in an equally smart and well-crafted paragraph, that my novel was among the worst things he had ever read. Each made a beautiful case. Each seemed to have a leg to stand on. Each was absolutely certain about the rightness of his opinion.

Doesn't this story prove the point that every "objective opinion" is an assertion of idiosyncratic personality and not anything like the truth? I once read a book that contained nothing but reviews of E.M. Forster's *A Passage to India*. To say that it included a range of opinions hardly captures the diversity of opinion expressed in those reviews. Brilliant and boring, humane and inhuman, slow and gripping, crystalline and impenetrable, there was nothing under the sun that wasn't said about that novel. Each reviewer had an agenda—some with Forster, all with life.

In our culture of winning and losing, the criticism we receive is that much more painful because we ourselves are rankers. The poet

Theodore Roethke once ran into the house of a fellow poet and exclaimed, "I believe that right now I am the number one poet in America, you are number two, and Robert Lowell is number three!" We might fervently wish to eradicate this desire to rank from our psyche, but it's hard to do in a culture that traffics in bottom lines and top dogs, best-dressed lists and blockbuster successes.

"So you are a great, terrible writer," my friend laughs.

"As are you." We clink glasses. "So what grade did your novel get—a C average?"

"Merde!" he exclaims. "Of course not! It got all those grades, every single one of them. You don't average those things. You live with all of them as if they were stars of varying intensities in a brilliant night sky. You live with the panorama and write on."

We drink to that. Between us we've written sixty books. We know.

# 13 | Three-Week Books

Georges Simenon, the Belgian novelist of Inspector Maigret fame—who lived and wrote in a Place des Vosges apartment—has always fascinated me, though a writer friend of mine dismisses him out of hand: "He was insane! And his daughter committed suicide because of some Electra thing." Both accusations are open to debate, as is Simenon's own claim that he slept with ten thousand women (the majority of them prostitutes, which must tarnish his boast anyway). What's not debatable is that Simenon wrote hundreds of novels, many of them in three-weeks' time. Three weeks! The concept of the three-week book fascinates me almost as much as Simenon's oeuvre does.

Simenon's slim psychological novels like *Sunday*, *November*, and *Monsieur Monde Vanishes* are tight, terrific investigations of human nature. Conceived to be slim, they're less than two hundred pages each. Simenon's habit was to check with his family doctor to make sure that he was fit for hard labor, then lock himself away for a disciplined, breathless three weeks-only, if his boast is to be believed, taking time out for sex. In those three weeks he would exhale a draft.

No doubt a majority of the books—even the slimmest ones—that any author pens will take months

or years to write. Simenon's feats, though, prove that there is no ironclad rule about how long writing a book must take. Therefore, it is entirely within reason to believe that you might go to Paris for a month, write up a storm, and depart with a complete manuscript. Isn't that something?

One year I was invited to give the keynote address at the Jack London Writers Conference. In preparation, I began making a list of the "wrong" things that writers say to themselves and the better things they might say instead. In essence, I prepared a short course in cognitive therapy for writers. I began writing my talk on a Tuesday and completed it that Friday. In the back of my mind an idea began to percolate: *I've spent a mere four days on this talk, which is already the nucleus of a nice, slim book. What if I commit to spending two more weeks on it—could I complete it in three weeks' time?* Years before, I'd had a small ghostwriting career. I'd written each of five books in two months' time or less. That had proven a snap. How much harder could writing a slim book in a mere three weeks be? A few thousand words a day, twenty-one days, and *voilà*.

The keynote address went well. Several literary agents in the audience approached me afterward, wondering if

When a novel is finished I have always the impression that I have not succeeded. I am not discouraged, but I see—I want to try again. I consider my novels about all on the same level, yet there are steps. After a group of five or six novels I have a kind of—I don't like the word "progress"—but there seems to be a progress. There is a jump in quality, I think.

—Georges Simenon

I intended to turn the talk into a book and, if I did, whether I had agent representation for it. Their reaction confirmed what I already suspected—that the material was marketable. I finalized the decision. This would be my first three-week book: conceived and completely written in three weeks' time.

For the next two weeks I worked on the book, and on a Sunday it was done. It came in at under 25,000 words—extremely short, not really a book at all, but functionally close enough—designed in such a way as to fill up 165 book pages. I sent the manuscript to one of my editors, someone who'd purchased books from me before but who'd also turned proposals down. She was not someone to buy just anything. She called a few days later to say that this was her favorite of my things. *Write Mind: 299 Things Writers Should Never Say to Themselves (and What They Should Say Instead)* had taken three weeks to write and a week to sell.

It is fruitless, guilt-producing, and counterpro-ductive to imagine that you can write a book in three weeks' time if that book must take three years to write. You can't compose *War and Peace* in a month. But isn't it an open question how much more quickly we might complete things if we challenged ourselves? Might not

there be a split second at the beginning of a project when we have the option of telling ourselves *three weeks* instead of *two years*? Aren't there tipping–point moments in the lives of our books when we might opt for a little more hare and a little less tortoise?

Simenon, asked repeatedly if he would ever write a "big book," always replied, "My big book is the mosaic of my small books." Maybe the big book that you've hoped to tackle is actually a series of smaller books, each one ready to fly off the spindle. Maybe this is the moment to think small and quick. There is as much beauty in slim books crafted quickly as in chubby books written over years. Paris might be the perfect place to try writing one.

# 14 | On Support

The issue of support is never very far from a writer's mind. Can you find a publisher—that's one kind of support. Can you pay the rent—how will you support yourself financially? Is your significant other supportive? This last question is especially provocative. Will your mate make faces when you say that you mean to write verse novels or that you consider journal-writing your art? Will he help you get published by keeping his eyes and ears open? When he learns that a friend of a friend knows a hot young literary agent, will he jump in and say "Get me that name!"?

This is how support is measured when artists make their tallies.

In 1908, a celebrated Rodin rented a ground floor studio in the Hôtel Biron, a mansion built by Gabriel in 1728 and transformed by the state into artist housing in 1905. In 1911, second-guessing itself about providing painters with such swell surroundings, the Ministry of Fine Arts evicted all the artists. Rodin, not wanting to leave his splendid digs, offered up his works in exchange for permission to spend his declining years right where he was. The state agreed, Rodin stayed on until his death in 1917, and today the Hôtel Biron is the Musée Rodin.

In the Rodin Museum you will find a room celebrating and commemorating the work of Camille Claudel—Rodin's student, assistant, and lover. The museum curators have done what Rodin would not do: acknowledge Claudel. There is no doubt that Claudel was a great artist—just look at her work, either in the Rodin Museum or on the Internet. Take a peek at her *L'Abandon*, *Clôtho*, *La Priére*, *Jeune Romain (Mon Frere)*, or *La Valse*. Compare these to Rodin's *The Thinker*, *The Kiss*, *The Burghers of Calais*, or his busts of Hugo and Balzac. I think you will agree that she deserved to be world-famous.

Instead she found herself institutionalized for the last thirty years of her life, having either gone insane or sunk into an impenetrable depression. Is it fair to say that her terrible decline was caused by Rodin's refusal to champion her work? Could be.

There are some simple tests to determine the essential soundness of an intimate relationship, and one is to ask whether each partner actively supports the other's dream of recognition. Anyone who shares a bed with you ought to support your efforts to write and get published. If he doesn't, he is failing you; and that failure may bite hard.

Diego Rivera, the most famous painter in Mexico in the early 1900s, ought to have shouted at the top of his lungs "Give Frida a show!" so that Frida Kahlo, whom he claimed was great, might have had her first show long before she did, when she was near death. A well-heeled, well-situated, well-connected Rodin should have announced to the world "Camille Claudel is every inch the real thing!" Whether that would have spared Claudel thirty years of institutionalization is beyond knowing. But as Phyllis Chesler put it in *Women and Madness*, "Some say that Claudel was a 'mad' genius who would have ended up the same sad way even if she had been nourished in a woman-loving family and culture. How can those cynics be so sure?"

Another famous couple from Paris mythology provide a counter-example. They are Anaïs Nin and Henry Miller—she of the famous journals, he of the

I, with a deeper instinct, choose a man who compels my strength, who makes enormous demands on me, who does not doubt my courage or my toughness, who does not believe me naive or innocent, who has the courage to treat me like a woman.

—Anaïs Nin

famous novels. Their story is full of everything that a legendary Paris romance ought to contain. There is their shared love for Henry's wife June, who regularly reappeared from America like a leitmotiv in a Wagnerian opera. There are the love letters and the lovers on both sides, Nin's pregnancy and the abortion, the black lace, the crises, the cruelties, the indecencies, the deep feelings. Theirs is a rich, painful, full-bodied saga.

Most relevant to our discussion is the way they supported one another. Nin paid for the publication of Miller's *Tropic of Cancer*. Miller fiercely championed Nin's diaries. He loved them, defended them, and wrote to a friend, "Never forget Anaïs's diaries. I haven't the slightest doubt that one hundred years from now this stupendous document will be the greatest single item in the literary history of our time." In an essay meant to help secure publication of Nin's journals, Henry declared, "Anaïs Nin has begun the fiftieth volume of her diary, the record of a twenty-year struggle toward self-realization. This monumental confession, when given to the world, will take its

It is not the fall of my second year in Paris. I was sent here for a reason I have not yet been able to fathom.

I have no money, no resources, no hopes. I am the happiest man alive. A year ago, six months ago, I thought that I was an artist. I no longer think about it, I *am*. Everything that was literature has fallen from me. There are no more books to be written, thank God.

—from the first chapter of *The Tropic of Cancer* by Henry Miller

place beside the revelations of St. Augustine, Petronius, Abelard, Rousseau, and Proust."

When Nin's diaries were finally published—expurgated at first, then in an uncensored edition—they indeed caught fire and became pillars of the feminist movement. By writing diaries and not novels, was she denying her talent or fulfilling her destiny? Both she and Henry wondered more than a little about that. Both feared that she might be squandering her talent on the diaries. But if privately Miller pressed her to write more fiction, publicly he championed the journals.

Whether you find yourself in Paris or Topeka, support your intimate other and look to him or her for support. You don't have to gush over your partner's every new poem, nor should you require that she gush over your every new story. But you and she will end up heartbroken if you haven't stood squarely in one another's corners. If you are together, you should fight for her, and you should expect her to fight the same good fight for you.

# The Pain of Perfect Little Parks | **15**

One afternoon I'm wandering Paris, having written
for a few hours at a café. I turn onto a narrow side
street, stroll a bit, and suddenly encounter a beautiful
postage-stamp-size park. Why is it there? Is it a relic
of Napoléon's plan to create a perfect city? The garden of some long-dead duke? Whatever it's doing
there, it is one answer to the question *Why come to Paris
to write?* You come because these splendid parks do not
exist in your neighborhood.

It is such a beautiful spot! Which makes it down-
right painful. The reason a perfect park pierces the
heart: Everyday life just isn't beautiful enough. A pic-
ture-postcard park of this sort speaks to that lack. The
mind instantly analogizes to other lacks: the gorgeous
novel you may never write, the joyous love you may
never find, the excellent writing career you may never
have. This beautiful park is an earthly delight and also
a slap in the face.

Despite its dangers, let me lead you to the exact
park I have in mind. Go to the Place des Vosges and
write. When you've finished, leave the square by the
northwest corner and turn right onto the Rue de la
Tournelle. In a few blocks the Rue de la Tournelle
becomes tuxedo row, with tuxedo hawkers lurking in

every doorway. Just before you get to the tuxedo sales-men, turn right onto the Rue Saint Gilles. Go a hun-dred feet down the Rue Saint Gilles, then turn left onto the dead-end-looking Rue Villehardouin.

This is the sort of street you might never take, because it looks so unprepossessing. At the end of the Rue Villehardouin the road jogs right, through an archway. Suddenly you will emerge on the Rue de Hesse. *Voilà*. At the intersection of the Rue de Hesse and the Rue du Grand Veneur you will find the Jardin Saint Gilles Grand Veneur, a perfect park and gar-den. It will take your breath away, the more so because it appeared out of nowhere, around a bend, off a street that suggested no wonders to follow.

Perhaps four or five young women from the shops will be sharing a picnic lunch. Perhaps the park's cat, black with a green collar, will wind through your legs. You'll find stone benches and the most beautiful trel-lised roses (trellis after trellis) as you sit surrounded by gorgeous, high-ceilinged, big-windowed apart-ments fit for royalty. Feel that complicated sorrowful joy that makes every creative person an Existentialist.

When we encounter masterpieces, we often expe-rience an identical pain. A piece of music makes us

want to cry—not because we feel joy, but perhaps because the music highlights our own mortality. Your own work, when you make it fine, may provoke this same prick of pain and come with an added danger—the fear that nothing else you do will ever seem (or be) quite as good. By creating something beautiful, you create something to compare your other work against. How many writers are measuring their current work against that unmatched piece from thirty years ago? Did depression regularly visit Hemingway when he mentally compared his latest short story to *A Clean Well-Lighted Place*?

I detest and despise success, yet I cannot do without it. I am like a drug addict—if nobody talks about me for a couple of months I have withdrawal symptoms.

—Eugène Ionesco

If your current writing turns out poorly, you have one pain to weather, the pain of failure. If it turns out beautifully, you have two pains to endure—the experience of a highlighted reality and the anticipation of future failures. How much amusement we must provide the gods! Beauty puts reality in stark contrast and sets the bar very high. If you are not writing, it is therefore important that you ask yourself the following question: *Am I afraid of beauty?*

Try not to allow this fear to develop into a phobia. Beauty has its dangers, but also its phenomenal rewards. Come to this perfect park—not to have your heart broken, but to write poignantly and well. Perhaps, close to tears, you will conjure something beautiful. Maybe this writing moment will haunt you down the road as you try to match the experience and the result, but it is still worth the gamble. By rejecting beauty, you may spare yourself pain, but you may also deny yourself a world of possibility.

One should only write when one has something important or profoundly beautiful to say, but then one must say it as simply as possible, as if one were trying one's best to prevent it being noticed.

—Stendhal

## Paris Parks

Parisian parks are blessed. They were invented for you, the writer—designed to embrace you, entertain you, and make you feel right at home. If the weather holds, write at least once every day in a Parisian park, varying your daily diet with venues off the beaten track. A day in the Place des Vosges or the Luxembourg Gardens is a given, but don't miss writing in the Parc des Buttes-Chaumont, the Parc Montsouris, the Parc de la Villette, or the Jardin des Plantes. Or the Parc Monceau.

The Parc Monceau is a beautiful, implausible park in the west of Paris, not far from the Champs-Elysées and the Arc de Triomphe, just off the Boulevard de Courcelles. It was designed two hundred years ago, by the artist and amateur landscape designer Louis Carmontelle (Carrogis), who received a commission from the Duc de Chartres to create a garden of dreams. Carmontelle created miniature interpretations of every conceivable architectural style. These architectural wonders, many of them fragments, include one and a half Roman pillars, a small Egyptian pyramid, and some stones resembling a miniature Stonehenge. At the very moment that you're certain that you've encountered every possible folly, you come upon a covered bridge, then a Dutch windmill, then yet another new extravaganza. You love them because they are the perfect size to be enjoyed as you sit on a bench writing. An actual coliseum or pyramid would fill the sky and blot out your dreams. These pint-size replicas make you imagine.

The benches in the Parc Monceau are of a particularly uncomfortable shape. Another folly! More rounded than your average bench, they are designed for form, not function. If you're a writer in Paris, you owe it to yourself to spend time in the Park Monceau, an army of gardeners clipping around you, children swinging in wrought-iron baskets for two beside you. If the populated lawns of the Place des Vosges look like Seurat paintings, so do the central fields of the Parc Monceau on any sunny afternoon.

# The Doable Dream

You may be worried about the cost of your dream. Is taking a writing jaunt to Paris within your budget? Almost certainly it is. You can live in Paris on $1,500 a month. If you can save or round up $4,500—less than the cost of many cruises and significantly less than the cost of a semester at college— you can spend three months writing in Paris. You will have to adhere to a certain regimen in order to live that modestly, but if you do, you'll have no trouble. Paris has always been inexpensive com-pared to other great cities.

Writing in a lovely park costs you nothing, and lovely parks are everywhere in Paris. Writing in the cool of a church costs you nothing, and churches are everywhere in Paris. By writing in free places, by eating more fruit than pâté, by drinking table wine and not vintage fare, and by searching out a cheap studio, a writer can build her book and spare her budget.

As to that studio, you can get started finding one by reviewing *FUSAC* (France USA Contacts), a free print and online magazine of classified ads for the English-speaking community in Paris. Here are some listings I found in a recent issue.

**FUSAC**
*www.fusac.fr*
Both English and French online versions are available.

• Montmartre, facing Sacré-Coeur, studio, panoramic views, elevator, balcony, available for ten months. 830 Euro/month.

• Marais Picasso, small studio apt under the roofs, bright, furnished, shower, kitchenette, for one year, one person. 650 Euro/month.

• Marais, renovated studio, lift, large terrace, bathtub, fully equipped, from two to twelve months. 850 Euro/month.

• Bastille, lovely, sunny flat, fully furnished, two persons, central heating, on courtyard. 570 Euro/month.

• Saint Germain des Prés. Charming, sunny,

*Paris Voice*
www.parisvoice.com

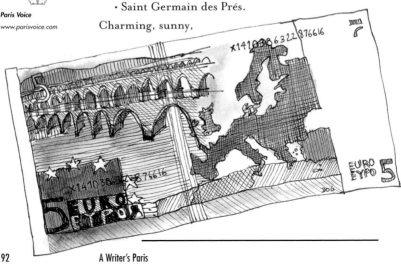

equipped studio, kitchen, bathroom, laundromat opposite. 740 Euro/month.

You should also check out *Paris Voice*, a magazine for English-speaking Parisians. The ads for housing in this magazine are similar to those in *FUSAC*. For example:

• Owner rents two studios completely renovated and newly furnished. Montparnasse and Bastille. 500 dollars, charges included.

• Paris apartment, 20th arrondissement. Père Lachaise studio, 22 sq. meters. Comfortable. No traffic noise. Marble bathroom, washer, large closets. Brand new equipped. Fine furniture. Ideal one or two meticulous persons. Nonsmokers. 800 Euro per month.

You can rent your studio before you leave the U.S., which is a fine option. The other approach is to land in Paris, stay at a cheap hotel or college dormitory, and begin to look around. You might even stay on at your cheap hotel if you find it livable and don't want to bother renting.

To find an apartment upon arriving in Paris, you would make use of one or all of the following resources.

• Pick up a current copy of *FUSAC* at a bookstore—in the Marais, for instance, you'd head to the Red

**American Church**
*www.acparis.org*

**Allo Logement Temporaire**
*www.allo-logement-temporaire.asso.fr*
You must e-mail, fax, or call in your request. A fee is charged for this service.

**De Particulier à Particulier**
*www.pap.fr*
This publication's Web site automatically translates apartment listings into English. Updated every 10 minutes on weekdays.

**Le Centre National des Oeuvres Universitaires et Scolaires**
*www.cnous.fr*
Each university town in France has its own regional office. This Web site, in French only, is hosted by the national organization, which you can contact before you arrive. Note that university accommodations in Paris fill up fast.

**Cité Internationale Universitaire de Paris**
*www.ciup.fr*

**Hostelling International**
*www.hostelbooking.com*

**Hello! series**
*www.helloeurope.com/france.htm*
The Web site companion to Margo Classe's series.

Wheelbarrow—and a current issue of *Paris Voice*, which can be found in hotel lobbies and bookstores.

• You might also walk over to the American Church on Quai d'Orsay, where you would find bulletin boards with housing listings.

• You could check with Allo Logement Temporaire on Rue du Temple, which offers apartment-finding help.

• If you understand French, you would get your hands on a copy of *De Particulier à Particulier*, the French-language bible for Parisian apartment hunters, available on Thursdays in print and a day earlier on the Internet.

As for temporary lodging to get you through the first week or two:

• You can find out about dormitories at French universities from Le Centre Regional des Oeuvres Universitaires et Scolaires (CROUS) on Avenue des Fleurs, and also from Cité Internationale Universitaire de Paris.

• There are at least a dozen hostels in Paris, of varying quality. It's best to research them online to decide if any will suit. You might start with the worldwide organization of hostels, Hostelling International.

• For cheap hotels, read the guidebooks. Highly recommended is Margo Classe's *Hello France!: Best Budget*

*Hotels in France*. Also, *Let's Go! Paris* and *The Rough Guide to Paris* are excellent resources.

In my wanderings, I encountered many cheap hotels that might do for your first few days. In the 19th arrondissement, on Avenue Mathurin-Moreau— a perfectly respectable street, with Jaguar and Land Rover dealerships down the block—I came upon the Antinea Hotel, with rates of 23 Euro a night without WC (toilet) and 30 Euro a night with WC (640 Euro a month for a room with toilet). I went in, asked to look at a room, and was told that they were full up— a good sign, I think.

In the 11th arrondissement, on a garment-district street (57 Rue Saint Sebastian, where the Boulevard Richard-Lenoir and the Boulevard Voltaire meet), I spotted a not very attractive but perhaps serviceable hotel with rooms at 23 Euro a night without and 39 Euro with WC. Outside, a sign read "We speak English." Everywhere I walked in the outer arrondissements, I noticed places in this low-end price range, many that I'd be willing to spend some nights at, others that I'd probably skip.

Spending several months in Paris writing, painting, or composing is an affordable, workable, doable dream. You will need to plan, which may be an undeveloped part of your nature. If you don't normally save, you will need to develop the ability to do so. Most importantly, you will need to risk and believe. If you can plan, save, risk, and believe, Paris is yours.

Once you are capable of planning, saving, risking, and believing, you can not only go to Paris—you can also make your writing dreams come true. You need to *plan* for your writing. You need to *save* time for your writing. You need to *risk* by getting your fingers tapping on the keys of your computer keyboard (or moving pencil along paper), despite the weight in your heart. You need to *believe* that you have something to say, that you will get it said by the third or fourth draft, and that it is useful, meaningful, and sensible to try.

Paris is a doable dream, and your writing is a doable dream. Both require the same nurturing and the same attention, the same courage and the same perseverance. Both come with a cost: Going to Paris requires some months of your time and some thousands of dollars; writing requires some years of your time, ugly drafts, nasty rejection letters, and bitter disappointments. Are these costs too high? Not for Paris, and not for a writing life.

## Researching Paris Online

The Internet allows you to research your Parisian writing jaunt before you go and keep your memories alive after you return. If you plan to stay for more than three months and therefore require a visa, if you intend to work (legit or underground), if you're looking for health insurance that will cover your Parisian stay—the Internet is the place to learn what you need to know. The information is free, readily available, and a mouse click away.

When you arrive home from your day job, fling off your clothes, get into your slippers and your Scotch, and zip around cyberspace. In no time you'll encounter the interesting statistic that 55,000 Americans reside in Paris. Doesn't that sound ideal? It's not so many as to make Paris America, but not so few that you can't contrive community. At **www.escapeartist.com** you'll hit upon the following morsel, provided by Jason Neiverth in the article "Teach English in France: Bon Chance, Mes Amis!":

EACH YEAR, THE FRENCH MINISTRY OF EDUCATION OFFERS 1,500 TEACHING ASSISTANTSHIP POSITIONS IN THE FRENCH PUBLIC SCHOOL SYSTEM EXCLUSIVELY FOR AMERICAN CITIZENS. CANDIDATES ARE HIRED TO TEACH 12 FLEXIBLY SCHEDULED HOURS PER WEEK OF CONVERSATIONAL ENGLISH. THE PROGRAM REQUIRES MINIMAL KNOWLEDGE OF FRENCH AS CLASSES ARE TAUGHT IN THE "TOTAL

IMMERSION" STYLE. THE PAY IS A
WHOPPING 900 EUROS A MONTH
(MORE IN SOME REGIONS) PLUS
SOCIAL SECURITY HEALTH CARE;
TYPICALLY ENOUGH TO COVER
BASIC EXPENSES IN ALMOST ANY
FRENCH REGION.

A site I particularly like is
**www.parlerparis.com**, hosted
by Adrian Leeds, who hosts
"Working and Living in France"
conferences where you can
learn about finding temporary
housing, dealing with technol-
ogy, setting up your finances,
and searching out employ-
ment. She publishes a
series of downloadable
e-books, among them
*Writers Insider Guide
to Paris* by Elizabeth Reichert,
who has worked in France as not only a free-
lance writer, but as an au pair, a literary tour guide, and a
painter's model. If you visit **www.parlerparis.com**, subscribe to

Adrian's twice-weekly e-mail newsletter (with a stunning photo in every issue).

As part of the "Working and Living in France" conference festivities, you can take a tour of Paris's twenty arrondissements with Thirza Vallois, author of the three-volume definitive guide to the Paris arrondissements, *Around and About Paris*. Her views are very similar to mine—and she has lived in Paris for forty years! She loves the 6th arrondissement (the heart of the Latin Quarter), speaks kindly of the eastern arrondissements, warns against the train-station-dominated 10th and the snotty 16th, is equivocal about the Marais, (which she finds beautiful but overrun), and is particularly partial to the 14th (her home arrondissement).

I think back. The 14th? Yes, the Parc Montsouris was an excellent writing haunt. I recall the cool shade of the Allée Samuel Beckett, a narrow street that runs straight down from the Parc Montsouris toward the Seine; and the market street, whose name I forget, dotted with cheap hotels and sporting one morning an American jug band playing "The Farmer in the Dell." Home to Man Ray, Modigliani, Henry Miller and the bones of Jean-Paul Sartre and Simone de Beauvoir in Montparnasse Cemetery, the 14th shines in memory.

Like me, Adrian is an encourager. She wants you to come to Paris. In one of her newsletters she writes about being a single woman in Paris.

I TELL YOU GIRLS, THIS IS THE GREATEST PLACE TO BE
SINGLE AND GET YOUR EGO BOOSTED ON A REGULAR BASIS.
TALL, SHORT, FAT, THIN, OLD, YOUNG, PALE, DARK,
BLONDE, BRUNETTE OR REDHEAD, MEN LOVE WOMEN AND
WOMEN LOVE MEN. AND SINCE MEN ARE SO MUCH LESS
THREATENING IN THEIR STYLE OF APPROACH, AND SINCE
PARIS STREETS ARE WELL LIT WITH SO MUCH LESS PERSONAL
CRIME, A WOMAN CAN BE ALONE AND FEEL SAFE AT ALMOST
ANY HOUR AND IN ALMOST ANY PART OF THE CITY.
BECAUSE IT'S SO ACCEPTABLE TO BE ALONE, TOO, A WOMAN
CAN SIT IN A CAFÉ ALONE, HAVE DINNER ALONE, GO TO A
MOVIE ALONE AND NOT FEEL CONSPICUOUS OR LONELY.
AU CONTRAIRE! SHE IS MORE LIKELY TO BE ADMIRED AND
APPROACHED BECAUSE SHE IS ALONE.

Come to Paris; and before you come and after you return, visit her via the Internet. You can keep abreast of Parisian events, current writing haunts and writers in residence, the latest art anecdotes and expat tales. Get in your writing first, of course; but right after you've written, hop an electron and make for the City of Light.

# 17 | The Professor of Nothing

The café is the writer's home. You can write at your desk, you can write at your cubicle at work, you can write—if you are a writer—anywhere. But cafés are your heaven. For the price of a cup of coffee, you get a table upon which to write, a lively scene to watch, and a thousand years of humanist tradition. A restaurant is for eating, a bar is for carousing, but a café is for creating. It exists for you and even because of you, as who else is free morning and afternoon to occupy its tables?

A café is yours even if you are blocked, under the weather, and bereft of ideas. Even then—especially then—it is your natural home and habitat. It is your home even if you only *wish* you were writing, even if you only *love* writing, even if you are only a fan, a hanger-on, a tourist in the arts.

I lunch with Emily, an American writer, at a café not far from the Sorbonne annex where English is taught. Many Americans gather at this particular café because of the Sorbonne connection. Emily explains to me that in their midst is a fellow, Bill, who is posing as a Sorbonne instructor. As she explains it, "And he is really a professor of nothing!"

Not that she or anyone else particularly minds. He acts as if he is employed by the Sorbonne, and they act as if he is not lying. They play along—not for sport, not so as to have an invalid to mock, not out of indifference or even out of compassion—but because impersonating a lecturer is a suitable role in a café setting. To rail against the arts, to act the Philistine, to side against ideas—that might get you the boot. But to want to be part of the scene so badly that you impersonate a literature instructor—that is pathetic, poignant, and perfectly acceptable.

"That's him!" Emily whispers, pointing to a table in the rear. Bill turns out to be a nondescript young man of thirty or so, a cheerful type engaged in a hectic monologue about some literary issue or other. Even at this distance I can hear "London Literary Supplement" and "outrageous point of view" and "post-Lacanian revolution." His tablemates do not roll their eyes or poke each other in the ribs. They just listen amicably.

"Who figured it out?" I ask. One of them with connections at

the college administrative offices confirmed that he had no Sorbonne association. By comparing notes, they realized that he spent his day moving from café to café. At each stop he kept to a certain routine. He would pull out a stack of "student papers"—the same stack each time—and studiously grade and regrade them. He would do that for an hour and then find someone with whom to chat—about literature, if he could move the conversation in that direction.

Emily and the others embraced Bill as perfectly suitable café company. A café is not a club, but it possesses clubby elements, and Bill belonged. An extension of the artist's living room and sometimes

his *only* living room, the café has been designated by all involved as the public home of not only the artist but of the artist manqué as well. Your only requirement for admission is to stand on the side of art.

Bill's acceptance is also commentary on the unimportance of titles and credentials in a café setting. If you can sketch, you can sketch. Who cares if you failed to graduate with a *beaux arts* degree? If you can write, you can write. Who cares if you never went to Princeton or Sarah Lawrence? If you can talk about literature—as Bill can—you get to talk about literature, whether or not you currently lecture somewhere. When you come to a café, you stand on equal footing with every art professor and Pulitzer Prize winner.

However, not every café is an artists' café. Some are too cliquey and claustrophobic. Some are too bustling and businesslike. Some are too much like bars or restaurants. Some are too sleek, too cavernous, too commercial, too empty. In some you are known too well, in some you are treated too rudely. Most just don't have *it*, that quality that distinguishes the artist's café from the others. As you stroll each Paris neighborhood, keep your eyes peeled. The right

The folly of mistaking a paradox for a discovery, a metaphor for proof, a torrent of verbiage for a spring of capital truths, and oneself for an orator, is inborn in us.

—Paul Valéry

café is worth its weight in gold. It is the place where you may spend half your time in Paris.

I learned later that Bill vanished. No one had actually been his friend, so no one knew what happened to him. Of the many possibilities, the least likely, I fear, is that he found a nice teaching post and is now a professor of something. More likely his money ran out and, with it, his charade. Maybe today he is working at a bookstore somewhere, or selling real estate, or retooling at law school.

If you're reading this, Bill, remember that you are always welcome back, just so long as you've retained your love of literature. There's always a place waiting for you at a café table somewhere. Cafés are a profound—even an essential—element of the writing life. If you have none nearby, it may be time to move.

*Disrespecting Albert Camus*

# Disrespecting Albert Camus | **18**

Like the great French novelist Albert Camus, you may
be a writer who finds yourself at odds with important
aspects of your culture and your community. Maybe
your politics are radically different from your culture's politics, maybe your beliefs are radically different, maybe you are better at detecting humbug and
wool-pulling than your neighbors. In that case,
two things are true: you will probably see it as your
duty to write as a cultural witness and speak out; and
those whom you speak out against
will probably not put up many
monuments to you.

   And so I supposed there would
be few monuments to Camus in
Paris. His World War II heroism
notwithstanding, he told too
many hard truths to receive public glorification. Out walking
one day in the northeast corner
of Paris, I discovered how the
politicians have decided to handle Camus. It did not surprise
me to find they have exiled him
far from intellectual Paris in

an unintended but ironic reminder of his short story collection *Exile and the Kingdom*.

The Place Albert Camus has been dropped on the shoulder of a busy traffic circle in an outer arrondissement. The Rue Albert Camus runs downhill from its namesake square through modern apartment complexes. The small, benchless Place is anchored by a chrome sculpture of a man who looks like a fleshless Terminator. Under this figure is the too-simple inscription "Albert Camus, journalist and writer." You would think that pride in one of your country's Nobel Prize winners and national treasures would outweigh the politician's usual animosity toward the truth. But no.

Albert Camus fared poorly in France. He was a real Resistance fighter, which didn't help, as too many of his fellow countrymen weren't. He doubted Communism, which made him the enemy of most French intellectuals, Sartre especially. He argued against religion, a position that fared better in 1780 than in 1950. Perhaps his greatest folly was arguing that Algerian Arabs and Algerian French might get along. While agreeing that colonialism was cruel, he asserted that expelling the French from Algeria was myopic and a cruelty of its own. That position sealed his fate as the darling of no one.

Camus was a dyed-in-the-wool skeptic, but refused to allow people to label him a skeptic just to dismiss him. Instead, he confronted his detractors with: "Since when is an honest man who refuses to believe the liar a skeptic?" He would have preferred a sweet humanism to chronic rage, but the times wouldn't permit it. He wrote in an open letter to a German friend that he was slow to credit the Nazi threat because he had hoped that Hitler was not as bad as he seemed—or, if he was, that Germans would come to their senses and oust him. He banked on hope, but finally had to admit his error. That is what a humanist does: He hopes that man will be better than he usually is, and sadly admits his mistake when man once again fails him.

On a recent trip to Paris I read Camus's last novel, *The First Man*. Published posthumously by his daughter, it was found in draft manuscript by the side of the road where Camus, a luckless passenger in a car driven by his publisher, was killed in a motor accident. It is an almost-wistful novel in which a mature artist, more than a little tired of wagging and pointing his finger, announces to his reader that life is not that bad. In *The First Man*, Camus explains that a poor child growing up in Algeria could get incredibly lucky, find himself befriended by a good-hearted teacher, and become Albert Camus.

It's a rags-to-riches story for thinking people, and not a romantic novel. We see the great divide that separated the French Algerians and the Arab Algerians; we see a child's fruitless search for a father he never knew. When Camus slips in an anecdote about a barber who slits the throat of the man he is shaving, simply because it has been too hot for too long, we know that he is reminding us that he can't write fairy tales.

Camus explained that "the nobility of the writer's occupation lies in resisting oppression, thus in

**First Lines of *The First Man***
Above the wagon rolling along a stony road, big thick clouds were hurrying to the East through the dusk. Three days ago they had inflated over the Atlantic, had waited for a wind from the West, had set out, slowly at first then faster and faster, had flown over the phosphorescent autumn waters, straight to the continent, had unraveled on the Moroccan peaks, had gathered again in flocks on the high plateaus of Algeria, and now, at the approaches to the Tunisian frontier, were trying to reach the Tyrrhenian Sea to lose themslves in it.

accepting isolation." You may think that you have come to Paris to fulfill a dream. Maybe you see your visit to Paris as a romantic gesture or a madcap fling. In fact, you are stepping into the shoes worn by our great truth-tellers. You are choosing an isolating experience—to witness in a land you don't really understand among people whose language you find beautiful but meaningless—for the sake of resisting everyday oppression. In every culture, the small-minded, the selfish, the power-hungry, and the corrupt stand ready to retaliate whenever a writer courageously announces,

An intellectual is someone whose mind watches itself.
—Albert Camus

"Here is what is really going on." The specter of their retaliation notwithstanding, we strive to say what we know to be true.

A government antagonistic to the truth (as are all governments) has isolated the memory of Albert Camus in an inglorious square in a nondescript part of town. It has added insult to injury by memorializing Camus with a chrome sculpture of an inhuman working man, a cross between Social Realism and Hollywood action figure. Not one tourist in ten thousand will end up at the Place Albert Camus by accident; not one in a million will end up there on purpose. But that is neither here nor there. The tragedy is not that Camus is insufficiently honored by his government. The tragedy is that he is not taught and not read.

# Gay Mayors | **19**

In our democratic, pluralistic society we stand committed to the ideas of tolerance and diversity. As a writer, you can celebrate these ideals by falling in love with a wide range of styles, genres, and subject matter and by tolerating your first (maybe awkward and feeble) attempts in unfamiliar territory. Maybe you suppose that you're only suited to write nonfiction even though you've harbored a lifelong urge to write a novel. Announce your own Fourth of July and free yourself from that unwarranted constraint by giving your novel a go.

It is a tribute to Parisians' commitment to tolerance and diversity that they elected a gay, socialist mayor. The Leftist Bertrand Delanoë, who in an interview two years before running casually revealed his sexual orientation, won a startling upset in a runoff election to become Paris's first openly gay mayor.

Among his first acts was to create a beach. Parisians are now treated each summer to the blossoming of a beach—complete with imported sand, palm trees, and beach umbrellas—along a two-mile stretch of the Seine. This annual event, running from mid-July to mid-August, has become quite the favorite, with Parisians twirling their parasols, lapping up the sun,

**Bertrand Delanoë** was born in 1950 in Tunisia and has served as Paris's mayor since 2001.

and assiduously avoiding the toxic waters of the river. A nice reward for opting for tolerance and diversity!

Rather more importantly, Delanoë liberated the grass. It used to be the case that you couldn't sit on the lawns of the Place des Vosges, the Parc Monceau, or other Parisian parks. Such frivolity was strictly forbidden, and the garden police, with legendary speed, would dart out from behind a clipped hedge to send you packing. This sad state of affairs prompted guidebook writers to warn that Parisian parks weren't suitable for children. Parks not suitable for children! The lawns of Paris's parks languished as manicured set pieces. Delanoë lifted that ban and freed the grass.

Parisians perhaps revere him more for instituting bus lanes, for cracking down (once again and as usual) on prostitutes plying the Bois de Boulogne, and for other civic improvements. But we must credit as his greatest feat returning the grass of Parisian parks to picnickers, idlers, children, lovers, and writers. This single change makes a writing trip to Paris worthwhile, as now the great urban parks of Paris have reached their full potential. You will see something that Lost Generation poets never got to witness: children playing on the grass.

When you elect a socialist mayor who professes that his favorite historical character is Robin Hood, what wonderful mischief you get. You get a mayor spending money from the city's luxury tax to buy up property in ritzy neighborhoods for conversion into working-class housing. You get bicycles for rent at métro stations, and streets closed to traffic on Sundays to accommodate strollers. Best of all, you get a lawsuit filed against Jacques Chirac (right-wing former mayor of Paris and president of France) and his exceptionally hungry wife for running up astronomical grocery bills at the taxpayers' expense.

What did these many good deeds net Delanoë? A long-bladed knife in the stomach. On October 6, 2002, during an arts festival, one Azedine Berkane stabbed Delanoë in the abdomen, announcing to police afterward that his religion taught that homo-

sexuality was unnatural and deserved punishment. Delanoë survived his wounds and gained twelve percentage points in popularity, another small but real victory for tolerance and diversity.

If the fact that Parisians elected a gay mayor doesn't make your head spin, get ready for this. Not long thereafter, Berliners followed suit and elected the openly gay Klaus Wowereit their mayor. At about the same time that Delanoë was leading sixty floats toward the Bastille in the Parisian Gay Pride Parade, Wowereit was heading a proud, snaking crowd of two hundred thousand, some in

Victorian garb, some in feather boas and leather, down Kurfuerstendamm Boulevard toward Berlin's Victory Column. Can't you just picture Hitler's expression?

Now, as you unpack your picnic lunch from your wicker hamper and spread out with your writing pad and your lover on the grass of the Place des Vosges, consider yourself celebrating tolerance and diversity. Go the next step and dream up a writing project so different from any you've previously contemplated that it constitutes a complete departure. Consider it your homage to the ideals of democracy.

# 20 | Rainy Day Lover

During the Paris winter, it can rain and rain. Weeks and months of a ferocious gloominess can descend, eradicating hope and the will to write, virtually extinguishing the City of Light, inspiring you to drink whiskey continuously. Even if you quit smoking five years ago, you may suddenly find yourself with a pack of Gitanes in your pocket. Even if you've fought your marijuana habit to a standstill, the old cravings may return with a vengeance. Watch out for the rainy season and what it can do to your nerves and your intentions.

You'll buy an umbrella. But a ferocious gust of wind will turn your umbrella inside-out and destroy it. Your second umbrella will meet a similar fate. Next you'll invest in some real rain gear, fancying yourself a Marseilles longshoreman during mistral. You'll budget for more hot chocolate and more café time and return to places that feel warm and inviting. You'll put in brighter bulbs in your room. You'll fight the urge to flee to the Spanish gold coast or some Mediterranean island. And, if the darkness hasn't destroyed your libido, you'll think about taking a lover.

My first time in Paris, I turned down sex out of shyness. Before it moved to the D'Orsay, France's collection of modern art was housed on the right bank at the Jeu de Paume, a museum that still exists and that today houses contemporary art. I was sitting in the café of the Jeu de Paume one afternoon, smoking a cigarette, when an attractive French

woman came a very long way from her spot among her friends, passing one smoker after another, to ask me for a light. I lit her cigarette but couldn't quite meet her eye. I still remember her smile. It said, "You fool. What do you suppose I'm doing here?"

But it wasn't just shyness. I had been married and knew about messes. My wife didn't make the mess and I didn't make the mess; we made the mess together. I knew that a lover would help with the rainy day gloom but perhaps at the terrific cost of opening the door to another dark relationship. Rainy day lovers, so warm, so delicious, also tempt us to give in to our shadow. They help us fall where we are primed to fall.

A writer in Paris told me the following story. Every day her husband would make a point of asking her, "When are you going to make some money at writing?" The only reply she could think to make was, "I'm trying." One day she sold a book for the quite decent advance of $15,000. She couldn't wait to tell her husband. He heard the news, sat down at the kitchen table, and made some calculations. "That comes to about twenty cents an hour," he said. "You're still a parasite."

Should he shoulder all the blame? No. We are co-conspirators in our miserable relationships. We each make more than half the mess, accounting for a mess larger than the sum of its parts. If we aren't writing and have decided to pick up a lover, that body beside us in bed is not the place to point the finger. We already weren't writing, were we?

The skies have darkened. The rainy season has begun. The broken window pane that amounted to cheap air conditioning in July is now letting in gusts of wind and rain water that puddles on the windowsill. You find that you've started picturing razor blades and nooses. Steady now! Run as fast as your shapely legs will take you to hot kisses and undressing in the gloom.

Just be careful. If her dramas begin to interest you more than your novel does, if evenings in his circle attract you more than your pen, if you throw over your writing life and blame him or her, slap yourself hard. It wasn't the rain; it wasn't your lover; it was your own secret wish to throw in the towel.

Love is good. Sex is good. Intimate relationships are good. Have these things. But if you happen not to be writing, do not glance even once across at your lover. Look in the mirror. It is never someone else's fault that we aren't writing.

# 21 | Eating an Elephant

The writer, quite possibly even better than the historian or the psychologist, knows that the trappings of civilization are but a thin veneer. The niceties of culture, the freedoms of speech and assembly, our useful legal proscriptions and social constraints—all can end in the blink of an eye if water gets scarce, if unemployment grows high, if fundamentalists multiply, if a despot gets his hands on the wheel. Any Renaissance can plummet into a Dark Ages. We have seen our excellent institutions remain intact for a few hundred years. Should we be sanguine that they will survive a few hundred more?

I am mulling this question over on a bench in the Jardin des Plantes, one of Thomas Jefferson's favorite haunts in Paris.

The **Jardin des Plantes** is the main botanical garden in France. It was originally planted as a medicinal herb garden in 1626.

A stone's throw from the elephants at the Jardin des Plantes zoo, it is an excellent location at which to speculate on the exact thickness of the veneer of civilization. To understand why this is the perfect place for such reveries, let me take you back to one of those endless spats between France and Germany.

These sparring neighbors grew close to war during the spring of 1870. On July 19, Emperor Napoleon III went off to fight the Prussians and was captured after several defeats. The Empress, no fool, fled to England as Parisians prepared to defend themselves against the Prussians. Thus began the siege of Paris. Crown Prince Frederick William wrote in his diary, "We shall certainly have to bomb Paris, but we might as well postpone that as long as possible, for I count definitely on starving out the city." Before too long, however, the Prussians decided to bomb as well. A program of bombardment and a program of starvation proceeded hand in hand.

To deal with dwindling supplies, Parisian butchers first refused to sell more than a day's ration of meat. Then the size of that ration shrank. Then there was no meat left. The first substitute was horse, from thoroughbred to mule. Then came dogs, cats, and

rats. Next came the zoo animals at the Jardin des Plantes, including Castor and Pollux, the zoo's two elephants. The only animals spared were the lions, tigers, and monkeys—the lions and tigers because they were too dangerous to approach; the monkeys, according to one account, "because of some vague Darwinian notion that they were the relatives of the people of Paris and eating them would be tantamount to cannibalism."

The veneer of civilization is exactly this thin and, when it cracks, we get dramas of the most poignant and horrible kind. You can always create a remarkable drama by imagining one of those veneer-cracking moments. It could be the moment when an anonymous French zookeeper, in love with his gazelles and wildebeests and forgetting that his animals are already prisoners and victims, defends his ménagerie against

the starving crowd. Or it could be *Lord of the Flies* or
*Animal Farm*.

If you're ever at a loss for a writing idea and want
to ensure that the stakes in your book are kept
sufficiently high, just scratch the veneer. At the level
of individual characterization, go for the id. Freud
posited a tripartite psyche made up of the ego, which
reasons; the superego, which wags its moralizing
finger; and the id, where our hungers and hatreds
dynamically reside. Just have your characters let loose
their id, as id is let loose in the classic science fiction
movie *Forbidden Planet*, and your readers will get all the
drama they can handle.

Janet Flanner, covering Paris for *The New Yorker*,
wrote in 1938 about Chamberlain's appeasement
speech: "War seemed imminent. Now all the French
know is that there is peace. In their curious calm, they
don't want to know anything else. It is the only thing
worth knowing, that and the knowledge exciting the
population of Europe—that statesmen can think
everybody's way out of war." Of course, they couldn't.
In every generation the same cracks inexorably appear.
The vigilant writer stands ready to report on these
recurring fissures.

# 22 | An Idea for a Novel

One young woman, a New York editor and would-be novelist, complained to me that Paris hadn't worked for her. Her room had roaches. She overpaid for bad cassoulet. Montmartre was tacky and Notre Dame impossibly crowded. Cigarette smoke assailed her in the cafés, and the roar of mopeds down the narrow Parisian side streets deafened her. Worst of all, she had fewer thoughts in Paris than at home in Manhattan. She stayed a full month, but hated it. Paris, she told me, had failed her.

I asked her the simplest question—the only question, really.

"Did you get up each morning, go out, and write?"

"No! No, I didn't." She sighed deeply. "I think I'm really more of an editor than a writer."

What did she mean? I imagine that she meant something like the following:

A Writer's Paris

*I'm a real writer, of course. But the whole writing thing is so difficult that I prefer to think of myself as a smart, capable professional—equal to sizing up manuscripts, better at wearing a suit than my ratty writing clothes, happier reading* Publishers Weekly *than quarterlies and chapbooks. I hate saying this and I don't even mean it, but the writing thing is so difficult that, imagewise and egowise, I am much better off presenting myself as an accomplished editor than as a failed writer.*

I asked, "What had you intended to write in Paris?"

"A novel. As usual. But no idea for a novel came to me."

"How did that work?"

"Excuse me?"

"The phrase 'I had no idea for a novel' could mean 'I kept my mind so full of chatter that no idea percolated up.' It could mean 'I had a ton of ideas for novels but none of them rose to the level of worth doing.' It could mean 'I've had this idea for a novel for years but it bores me and I can't seem to get past thinking about it to some better idea.' It could mean—"

"I get it! I don't know. I think I literally mean that I had no idea for a novel. Nothing came to me. Nothing."

"And what do you take *an idea for a novel* to mean?"

"God! Can't you ask any easy questions?"

I am finding it very hard to get my novel started. I suffer from stylistic abcesses; and sentences keep itching without coming to a head.

—Gustave Flaubert,
on beginning
*Madame Bovary*

What is an idea for a novel? I think we'd agree that the seed for a novel exists in every conversation we overhear and in every stray sight we see. This is true whether we find ourselves in Paris or in Boise, whether the conversation or sight is dramatic or undramatic, whether we encounter it early in the morning on the way to work or late at night in our dreams. We see a taxi driver get out of his cab and he is wearing a certain expression—a novel could get woven around that look. Our friend tells us a story about an insult she received—a novel could get woven around that insult. There are ideas for novels everywhere, since a novel is just the stuff of life organized and punctuated in the writer's idiosyncratic way.

So the problem ought to be that we find ourselves flooded and overloaded by too many ideas for novels, not too few, since fictional possibilities exist abundantly and endlessly. By what mysterious process do all these ideas evade the writer-to-be? Why is she not snapping her fingers eighteen times a day, crying "*That* could be a novel!" and "*That* could be a novel!" and "*That* could be a novel!"? What's going on?

The problem is probably something that you may never have heard of before, something that I like to call *void mind.*

Long ago the Buddhists identified *monkey mind* as a common cognitive state. The mind, given free reign by our defensive structure to drown out our real thought with endless yammering, chatters incessantly as a monkey chatters in the trees. But I believe there is a second state, just as common as monkey mind, that serves the same function of separating us from our real thoughts.

*Void mind* takes over where monkey mind leaves off. It is a defensive state of silence we create that leaves us feeling woolly and foggy. Sometimes we drown out our ideas with incessant noise, and sometimes we drown them out with eerie silence.

You may be unfamiliar with void mind as a concept, but very familiar with it as a reality in your life. In Paris you might experience monkey mind and void mind in sequence as follows. First you berate yourself for all the tourist sites you haven't adequately covered. You nag yourself about spending too much money on dinner every night and for leaving your garden back home untended. You follow one monkey-mind harangue with another. Then, as if you could possibly be in the right frame of mind to create, you exclaim to yourself, *Okay, time to write!*

Suddenly silence descends. Exhausted by your self-battering, anxious about your writing, you find yourself staring at the blank wall of your studio without a single thought in your head. Void mind holds sway. You feel as if you're at the bottom of a well, or lost in outer space. This silence is so deafening that you rush out to see another two rooms of the Louvre. Later that night, tired and disappointed, you agonize some more about how it is that you have no ideas for a novel.

I do not say any of this to the editor who felt Paris failed her, because she is in a rush and must dash off to do New York things. If she had the time, I'm sure she'd understand. But who has the time? She has many professional things to do, some of which are even for my benefit, so it is probably better for me that she is not in Paris writing her novel. Is it also better for her? Quite possibly. Until she realizes what having no ideas for a novel signifies, she won't have any ideas for a novel. I hope the day will come when she recognizes that ideas are plentiful—but so, damn it, is the anxiety.

## Elusive Books

Sometimes the distance between an idea and a book is short and easy to traverse. You have an idea, you sit down at the computer, and you are off and running. Other times, the book eludes you. The idea may be crystal clear, and yet the way to spin the idea into a 75,000-word narrative won't come. Indeed, this may happen with your very favorite idea and keep you hanging for years as, every so often, you take another stab at alchemy. You write 1,000 words or 10,000 words and discover that the form to contain the spark is still eluding you.

One cloudless morning I'm out and about at nine. Paris is quiet. I head toward Montmartre, crossing the Paris garment district on my way to the steps below Sacré Coeur, where I intend to write. Street after street of wholesale and retail clothing stores mark the way from the Marais to the Mountain of Mars. At every second street corner, a group of young men with trolleys—the bellhops of the district—wait for the arrival of truckloads of raw fabric and finished clothes. These clusters of men remind me of my own neighborhood in San Francisco, the Mission District, where Spanish-speaking day laborers wait on street corners for contractors to grab them up for bathroom remodels.

As I cross the garment district of Paris I am suddenly struck by a thought. What about Darwin's wife? I stop dead in my tracks. Behind every great man, the old saw has it, is a great woman. What about behind every great idea? What if Darwin's wife is both an interesting character and crucial to the birth of evolutionary thought? What if their relationship is dynamic and telling? Darwin waited twenty years to publish *The Origin of Species*. Is it possible that his wife played a role in that delay? Or did she push him to publish? First of all, did he have a wife?

A second thought strikes me. Maybe this is the way I can write that damned book. A book has been eluding me for twenty years. I want to demonstrate that religion is a betrayal of humanity. But the way to say that over tens of thousands of words has eluded me. Now it strikes me like a hammer blow: What if my argument can be embedded in a charming tale about Darwin and his wife? I turn on my heels and rush toward my favorite Internet café, located in a back corner of the Marais.

As I hurry across Paris I find myself thinking of *The Day The Earth Stood Still*, that classic science fiction movie. Its makers hoped to tell a cautionary tale about the probability of an apocalypse, given our weapons of mass destruction and our careless hatreds. At one point, the hero from outer space has been killed by soldiers but is brought back to life by his bodyguard robot, who has some healing tricks up

his sleeve. The hero, alive again, is asked by the startled heroine, "You mean that your robot has the power of life and death?" Our hero pauses, not for effect, but to check over his shoulder to see if the Hollywood censors are listening.

They are. The moviemakers intended the hero to reply simply, "Yes." That would have been a wonderful moment—a look forward to cloning and a lovely anti-theistic accent in a culture steeped in soupy piety. Shouldn't that yes have slipped under the radar screen of the studio censors? But the censors never sleep. "You can't say that," they warned. "If you do, we'll kill the picture." In the finished product, we hear the hero say, "No. That power resides in the hands of the Almighty. This technique, in some cases, can restore life for a limited period."

My mind is racing. That anecdote and Darwin's wife may connect. At the Internet café I grab the last computer, and the first thing I locate is an eloquent letter from her to her husband. I learn that a much-loved daughter died young and that neither of them got over her death. They are real parents, real lovers, real people, Mr. and Mrs. Darwin. Is Emma Darwin the door into my diatribe book? I can't say yet. I am supremely happy visiting with Charles, Emma and the ten little Darwins, but no bell has tolled to signal that this elusive book is now ready to be written. Maybe it has; or maybe it will take another decade. Whichever it is, I will not give up the chase.

# 23 | Smaller and Smaller

Smaller and Smaller

Once you're in Paris, you will probably end up living in a tiny studio to keep expenses down. You can certainly survive in a small studio, just as millions of artists have done from time immemorial. But there is a catch. The smallness of your studio will definitely grate on you. Cheap rooms and the things that come with them—the alienation, the bad dreams, the roaches, the dingy walls, the ratty furniture, the unbroken silence—addle the brain over time. One afternoon you'll find yourself daydreaming about wide verandas. Then, rather more dangerously, you'll think about proposing marriage to the next person you meet who has a *real* apartment.

I once lived in a room that was also being used by the building's owner as a storeroom. That shoebox contained seven wardrobes, three drop-leaf tables, two standing mirrors, and a mattress on the floor that you fell onto as you entered. Its only saving grace was a small table by the window where I could breathe and smoke Camels. To preserve my mental health, I developed a ritual entrance, a ceremonial dive onto the mattress when I entered. That ritual dive—going *with* the absurdity of the situation, rather than *against* it— made all the difference. Humor helps.

The sole cause of man's unhappiness is that he does not know how to stay quietly in his room.
—Pascal

In another apartment, the oversized bathtub in the bathroom proved more accommodating than the adjoining room. I therefore used the bathtub for living. Sometimes I did the dishes there, sometimes I read—*avec* or *sans* water—sometimes I wrote, sometimes I entertained. Put two pillows and a candle in a bathtub, and you guarantee memories. The room I can hardly remember; but, oh, the bathtub. Make use of your room's best feature, which may be its balcony or its writing niche. If it has no good features, pretend that it does. Pretending helps.

I asked some writers in Paris what they did when their cramped quarters started to addle them. Some went out, day or night, and walked until exhausted. Others used the café down the block as their living room. Some called friends back home and left their room via the telephone. Others gave in to the feeling and cried until the mood passed. Most used Paris like an extension of their living quarters, the Village Voice bookshop becoming their personal library, the Tuileries their personal garden.

That's the best answer: Stay out all day. Use Paris. Write out, rather than in. Find a home café, or several. Find a bookstore with comfortable seating. Make

some friends. Go back to your room only when you find it absolutely necessary; which, if you strike it lucky, may not be for days on end. Use your room as you would a bathroom—as a necessary convenience, as better than outdoor plumbing or nights under a bridge. In the winter, when the rains come, this will prove more difficult. Then you'll need extra candles, extra chocolate, and music with a beat.

Prepare for the onslaught of strangeness by pledging to remain passionate and ambitious no matter how cramped your room begins to feel. Your very ambitiousness can inoculate you and save you. Georges Rouault, filling his studio with one unfinished painting after another, cried to his loving daughter, "How am I ever to manage?" She replied, sensibly enough, "Why not try to finish three or four of them?" But small rooms do not make for small agendas. "No!" he replied. "I will finish 133 of them!" Even if your room is shrinking daily, your ambition can buoy you.

Another antidote is making friends with people who live in real apartments. I visited some expats on the Boulevard Richard-Lenoir and their apartment was American-size, with room after spacious room—one even sporting huge beanbag chairs. When you sat

down at the kitchen table, your back was not directly up against the wall. Make at least one such friend, and drop in whenever your walls close in on you.

Small rooms are not death sentences. We have all written in them, and most of us have survived them. Solitary confinement can turn a warrior to jelly, but out of those small rooms have come the melodies that enrich lives, the paintings that break traditions, the novels that bear witness. We tolerate those threadbare rooms and maybe even revere them, their real dangers notwithstanding. We make sacrifices for our art. If a too-small room in Paris is the greatest sacrifice you ever have to make, thank your lucky stars.

## Blue Marais

One summer I rent a studio in the Marais, on the narrow Rue Saint Gilles, in the heart of gay, Jewish, touristy Paris. My landlord's aide arrives and guides me through the front hall, past a courtyard, through a door beside an old-fashioned urinal, and up several narrow, steep flights of steps to my attic studio. She is new to her job and hasn't seen this studio before. She takes one look around, shakes her head, and exclaims, "So Marais!"

The tiny, under-the-eaves studio is done entirely in blue, mostly that heartbreaking Mediterranean blue that you see in posters of Greece. Its high-up windows—virtually skylights—are framed in blue. The exposed beams are painted blue. The built-in desk/bookshelf combo is blue. The bedside lamp and its shade are blue. The trim around the curtained opening between the main room and the kitchen is blue. The art on the wall is blue: Matisse's blue women cutouts.

That's not all. The blankets are blue. The light fixtures are blue. The door to the apartment is blue. The dining table has blue legs and blue grout between the white tiles on its surface. Next to the sink, a small painting of the muscled back of a man (this being a gay section of Paris), is blue on blue. The phone is blue, the coffee pot is blue, the framed postcard above the stove is of a blue café. Even the iron is blue!

All this blue puts me in mind of monochromatic painting. Paris herself does the same. The summer I rent my blue Marais studio, red is the color in Paris. Virtually every product in every shop window is red, as is almost every stitch of clothing for sale, every gallery exhibition, every advertisement. Chinese reds and cadmium reds inflame Paris. Alexander Calder once exclaimed, "I love red so much I almost want to paint everything red!" Paris this summer is a Calder dream.

You quite expect to see Yves Klein, patron saint of monochromatic painting, wandering Paris, stopping at every boutique window, and nodding thoughtfully. "Once the adventure of the monochrome started, my fine senses found their way," Klein remarked. How well-oriented he would have found himself in an all-red Paris.

Does monochromatic painting analogize to the writer's craft? I wonder. Is there a useful relationship to draw between the artist's palette—dubbed a magical laboratory by the painter Arturo

Fallico—and the writer's vocabulary, equally alchemical? Is there something like a novel in the Dutch palette, a short story in the colors of Provence, an all-red poem? I think there is, but the bridge from the one discipline to the other eludes me at this second.

It can take time, often a very long time, to gestate a piece of writing. You have the sense that there is a connection between this and that, but the connection is not yet available to you. You want to say something about the relationship between energy, mass, and the speed of light, but you just don't have the right understanding. How do you get to that right understanding? You get there—if you ever do—by not wavering, by muddling along, and by writing what is available.

You may not be able to write novel A because you are not ready for it or because it is not ready for you. Therefore you settle for writing novel B or nonfiction book C or personal essay D or article E, work that may feel pale compared to that beautiful but unavailable novel A. Novel B or article E, however, has the virtue of having arrived at term; it can now be born, so you birth it. In this way, you create a body of work while at the same time standing in the right relationship to all your beautiful work still to come.

One day I may know what I want to say about all-red novels and all-blue nonfiction. Until that day, I write what I can.

# Picasso's Ghost | **24**

Beauty is such a tricky business. First of all, we are built to appreciate it. Appreciating beauty is a genetic matter, part of our biological makeup. When you turn to your lover and whisper, "Isn't that a gorgeous sunset?" you are posing a rhetorical question. You have no doubt but that your lover agrees. If your lover were to reply, "No, what's beautiful about it?" you would presume that an alien had taken up residence in his or her body—an alien or a French Structural Postmodernist.

As postmodern people, we have rightly learned to be suspicious even of our genetic inclination to find the beautiful beautiful. Who or what might be making a fool of us and using our innate sense of beauty against us? Might that gorgeous sunset not be the direct result of five-alarm smog? Certainly. Correctly suspicious, we're forced to deconstruct beauty and exclaim, *Don't try to fool me with beautiful things! Maybe that prose is beautiful, maybe that face is beautiful, maybe that commercial is beautiful, but so what? It's probably just some sort of gimmick!*

We want to stand wholeheartedly for beauty, but we know that we can't. We know too much. That knowledge, very much like the knowledge of good and evil, plays psychological tricks on us. Understanding the power of beauty to seduce and manipulate, to mean nothing, we get a little grumpy and a little feisty and come close to advocating for ugliness.

Out of precisely such feelings emerged modern art. Modern artists painted images of urinals not because they were in love with urinals, but because they couldn't stomach the easy glory that an iris or a sunset would have garnered. They wanted to earn their sense of heroism, and not have blue ribbons handed to them because they could imitate Bouguereau or Fantin-Latour.

When (as you certainly should) you visit the Centre Pompidou, Paris's outlandish contemporary art museum, keep this in mind. Every artist featured there could have painted an image of an iris or a sunset. Instead you will see odd and sometimes eloquent work that only makes sense in the context of Deconstruction.

Of the more eloquent variety is a sardine can bed—a sardine can the size of a queen bed. This oddity so amused my daughter Natalya and me that we searched high and low in the gift shop for a postcard reproduction. Not spotting one, we had to commit a tourist misdemeanor: I distracted the guard while Natalya snapped a picture.

The **Centre Pompidou** has arguably the leading collection of contemporary art in Europe. Even if you're not a fan of the art itself, you'll enjoy the unique architecture of the building—the escalators are on the *outside* of the structure, rather than the inside. Open unusually late, you can stroll the exhibits from 11 a.m. to 9 p.m., except on Tuesdays, when the Pompidou is closed.

Then, laughing, we made our escape down the
outside escalator with its spectacular views of Paris.
Below us, hundreds of tourists thronged the vast concrete expanse fronting the museum, some of them
surrounding a band of Andean flautists, another con-
tingent captivated by a man with parrots, a third
group encircling an old-fashioned sword-swallower.
We made our way through the crowd to the Stravinsky
fountain with its dancing G clefs and spinning bowler
hats, found a café table, and ordered hot chocolate.

No doubt you, too, will find yourself at this exact
spot. In almost no time you'll sense a presence

nearby—the ghost of Pablo Picasso. Barrel-chested, bull-headed, Picasso does not appear for the tourists. For you, however, he is the ectoplasm hovering nearby muttering "Beauty! Beauty! Beauty! What a business!" Relax and accept his presence. His message is the right one. You must champion meaning, not beauty, because it is the better bet—or the lesser absurdity.

As you sit at your café table across from the Pompidou, enjoying the antics of the fire-eaters and the tourists, pull out your writing pad. That gesture is as eloquent today as it was before beauty came with a question mark. Just be careful. Narcissus made his mistake at the water's edge. Do not make yours with your pen in hand. Write beautiful sentences, if you like—but make sure to say what you mean.

A Writer's Paris

## From Renoir to Picasso: Artists I Have Known by Michel Georges-Michel

One day a certain painter in Montparnasse came to see me with one of Picasso's canvases. He wanted only a modest price for it, but he insisted on my getting Picasso to verify it. I took it to the latter, who gave one look at it, and said crossly, "It's a fake."

"But I'm sure it's a genuine Picasso," my visitor protested to me the following day. "Here's another one. Doesn't that strike you as genuine too?"

"It certainly does."

But when I showed it to Picasso, he glanced at it even more cursorily and said, "It's a fake."

By now I began to have some doubts myself. So I took one of my own Picassos down from the wall, and carried it to the Rue de la Boétie for the artist to pass judgment. And again he stated flatly, "It's a fake."

That was too much, and I exclaimed, "But I saw you do this canvas myself!"

He gave a slight shrug. "Oh, well," he said with a smile, "I sometimes do fake Picassos myself."

# Not Writing | **25**

It is one thing not to write at home. At home you can keep yourself busy with the rigors and routines of ordinary life and not quite notice that you aren't writing. There is always another errand to run, another meal to prepare, another corner of the garden to weed. Time is abundant and easily squandered, and also fleeting and hard to grasp. There is always tomorrow, but never today.

It is another thing, however, to not write when you've come to Paris to write. That's a failure much harder to ignore, albeit a common one. One in a hundred writers comes to Paris and writes up a storm. The other ninety-nine arrive and fall into a nonwriting routine. They wander the streets and feel their hearts bursting, but (except to jot down the occasional impression) rarely pull out their pads.

One day of not writing is nothing. Two days are nothing. The occasional sick days, blue days, play days, and days of pure idleness are nothing. But the I-haven't-written-in-two-weeks-and-I'm-not-even-close-to-writing not writing—that's intolerable. Each day spent that way is a new reproach and buries you deeper in a pit of regrets. The deeper that pit grows, the less possible it feels to claw your way out.

One day you shake your head and realize that you've given up the ghost.

Not writing may dog you from home, where you were already not writing. It may creep up on you as your Paris days unfold. Maybe you came to Paris, had your share of lovely times and crises, and actually managed to write—though not as much as you had hoped. Paris turned out to be rainier and lonelier than you expected, and fewer days found you thinking about your novel. You got sick once or twice, recovered, had a money scare, had some lovely times by the Seine, and, one day, completely stopped creating. You went off traveling to the Normandy coast with some new acquaintances and got embroiled in their interpersonal dramas. It was sexy and wild, but also stupid. Then you spent a week obsessing about the tall waitress (or was it the slim waiter?) at the corner café. After that obsession ran its course you got caught up following a lurid current event on television, the abduction of a schoolgirl from her Paris apartment. You sat glued in front of the television for a week, manically flipping channels for updates. If you were writing, you would never have succumbed to such a distraction. But you weren't writing.

Now you haven't written for two months. Several of those days you spent entirely in bed. You really don't feel well, mentally or physically. You attribute your not writing to your low-grade illness and announce to yourself that you haven't the "necessary equilibrium" to write. You feel scared, scared that this downturn may be permanent. For the first time since you arrived in Paris you've begun thinking about heading home early, your nonrefundable ticket be damned.

What will you do? What can you do?

First of all, cry. Really cry. Feel as sad as you actually feel. Cry because you're lonely, because you've spent too much money, because you hate the novel you're writing. Really sob! Better a wild thunderstorm than month after month of dreary weather. Feel genuinely sad and not routinely depressed. Feel!

Then make a plan. Let it be short and sweet. For instance: Get up, even if you don't feel like it. Get dressed, even if you don't feel like it. Gather up your writing, even if you don't feel like it. Go to a café, order a croissant and coffee, open up your pad and write, even if you don't feel like it. Maybe you hate your current novel: Love it by writing. Maybe you have no idea what comes next in the novel: Learn by writing. Maybe you want to quit: Persevere by writing. The plan in a nutshell: Get up, go out, and write.

If you make it to the café and manage to write, celebrate with a second croissant, some extra butter and jam, and a second cup of coffee. Say "I will do this again this afternoon, and tomorrow morning, and tomorrow afternoon." Slam the table top for emphasis. "I will do this again this afternoon, damn it!" Then smile. Your heart is beating again. Your blood is boiling. You have a pulse, a future, a brain that works. You've come back from the dead.

Look around you. Isn't it a different Paris? I bet it is. Even magical places lose their allure when you abandon your art. The Seine becomes just another toxic open sewer, Notre Dame just another pile of chiseled stones. Then you manage to write for an

hour
and the magic
returns. Paris smiles again.
The City of Light lives up to its name.
You dance back to your cramped studio.

If you've come all the way to Paris to write and
you're not writing, don't capitulate. Prove the exception. It is common not to write, and unusual to
return to the trenches. You can be among the ninety-
nine who regret, or you can be the hundredth who
writes. You can return from Paris with excuses or with
a manuscript. Which will it be? Shed salty tears, pack
up your notebook, head to a café, and find your way
back to your writing.

## Once You've Written

You could hunt for a souvenir. Just a block from the Centre Pompidou there is a shop full of beautiful glass—a shop as scary as it is beautiful. It is scary—or at least was, on the day that I visited—because the fellow on duty, having slept with many Marais men and not having sorted that all out, kept dropping the piece of glass he was dusting each time an old lover entered. This nerve-racking scene repeated itself five or six times during the twenty minutes I spent choosing between the orange bud vase and the blue one. A bull in a china shop would have done more damage than this anxious clerk, but the carnage would have ended much more quickly. I suggest that you not drop by there.

You could wander over to Place de la Madeleine and Fauchon and lunch on cold roast chicken at the stand-up counter. The price of this stand-up lunch is quite likely to please, at least in relation to the staggering prices attached to the whole glazed ducks with fruit, the poached fish in aspic, the smoked salmon, the kiwi tarts, and

the spectacular pâtés carefully displayed in the windows. Those would break your budget and cause you to return stateside this very afternoon. So, some cold roast chicken is a distinct possibility.

Or you could visit the Jardin des Poètes, where poems by Corneille, Racine, Baudelaire, and Apollinaire are placed among the flower beds. You could finally get to the Louvre and catch a little Hieronymous Bosch and Jan Van Eyck. You could gawk at the nine hundred musical instruments at the Musée de la Musique while listening to musical excerpts and verbal explanations through headphones. You could visit the Salvador Dali Museum (L'Espace Dali); or the Musée de la Chasse et de la Nature, a hunting museum perfect if you fancy stuffed animals with glassy eyes; or the Musée du Vieux Montmartre (Museum of Old Montmartre), complete with a re-creation of a nineteenth-century café.

There is still Shakespeare & Company, which moved some years ago to its present location just across from Notre Dame. No doubt you will visit it. Upstairs is a tiny museum. One Sunday I posed my daughters, aged 20 and 18 at the time, on a divan in a mirrored room lined with bookshelves. I had them sit archly and read an old, dusty book, looking like bored daughters in a Jane Austen novel. Then I led them on a wild goose chase up the back stairs, imagining that the tiny museum continued somewhere. It doesn't.

Here's a better idea. Cross the 12th arrondissement to the Bois de Vincennes. There is something along the way that you really shouldn't miss. If you're strolling along Avenue Daumesnil, a straight path to the Bois, you will notice something high above you that reminds you of elevated tracks. Every so often you will spot a flight of stairs leading up there. Climb right up! What you will encounter is the Promenade Plantée, located above the Viaduc des Arts. This promenade is a joy and a revelation: roses, cherry trees, and dozens of artisan boutiques and galleries sprouting under the archways of a defunct railroad.

You could certainly go there! But first you must write. You handle nagging doubts most effectively by calmly and religiously writing. Fauchon or the Promenade Plantée will make for a wonderful destination, but not until you have gotten in two hours of writing. It will be splendid to catch a last museum or boulevard, but it will please you even more if you can say "I worked well right up to the last minute."

Your writing done, you can make your pilgrimages—an elaborate one to the gardens of Versailles or the top of the Eiffel Tower, a simpler one to the shops around the Centre Pompidou for a classic poster or a CD of café music. You can catch a crepe, sip a hot chocolate, wander down a narrow street. It hardly matters what you do, once you have written.

# Second Chances | **26**

Often quoted to make a point about American culture and character is F. Scott Fitzgerald's famous
line "There are no second acts in American lives."
In fact, nothing could be further from the truth.
We are not done at twenty, thirty, forty, or fifty; we
have not ruined our chances by not writing for a
decade; we have not precluded the possibility of a
second act and a second chance by making even the
worst mistake. Alcoholics get sober, cowardly lions
find their courage, and with each new dawn, every
writer gets a second chance to write well.

Paris herself, on the brink of destruction, got a
second chance. Toward the end of World War II,
Hitler had his engineers mine the bridges of Paris.
Explosives were placed beneath the Invalides, the
Assemblé National, Notre Dame. The Eiffel Tower
was rigged to topple into the Seine. All that was need-
ed for Paris to explode was a command from the
German commander in Paris, General Dietrich von
Choltitz. In love with Paris, von Choltitz never gave
that order.

As the Allies approached, Hitler badgered von
Choltitz from Berlin. "Is Paris burning?" Hitler
screamed. Von Choltitz offered up one excuse after

another. An apoplectic Hitler pestered and threatened von Choltitz, who stood his shaky ground. Finally the Allies arrived to an intact Paris. Nothing could have been more appropriate than, years later, France awarding von Choltitz the Légion d'Honneur.

Often your second, third, or fourth chance only arrives because you have made a heroic decision to persevere. When an arthritic Matisse could no longer paint, he began to create cutout collages that are now world-famous. Solving the problems of how and what to create with crippled fingers was a real task, but the most important task he faced was not giving up. When your editor tells you that your sequel is not wanted because the sales of your first book do not justify the risk, you only get a second chance by courageously doing the next thing. You must convince this publisher, or find another publisher, or publish the sequel yourself, or write something different. The choices are straightforward enough. All that's required is fortitude.

I'm reminded of this as I stroll with my acquaintances Sally and Meredith through the Jardins du Luxembourg. The day is splendid; the puppet show is crowded; the Grand Bassin is sporting its toy sailboats; the pony path is busy. The 150 palm trees and orange trees, returned from winter storage, are blissfully sunbathing, as are the 350,000 flowers that get planted or transplanted each spring. We pass *Art*, *Time*, *and Glory* paying their allegorical tribute to the statues of Delacroix and Saint Geneviève (the patron saint of Paris, who appears to be doing her job nicely). I'm telling Sally and Meredith the story of an unexpected second chance in my writing life.

I'd done three successful books with a publisher. I was feeling my oats and proposed an ambitious book in which I meant to attempt nothing less than a complete philosophy of life. The publisher offered me a nice advance and said *Go for it!* I then proceeded to make a hash of the book. A few weeks after I turned in the manuscript, I heard from my chagrined editor, who lamented that there was no way her house could publish the

book. It was so far from where it needed to be that all they could do was cancel the contract.

I hated the fact that I had ruined my relationship with this publisher more than I hated that I had ruined this particular book or this particular deal. It seemed inconceivable to me that they would give me a second chance. Indeed, they passed on my next several ideas, apparently confirming my fear. But, as they hadn't locked the door, I never stopped trying to reenter. Over the next few years I pitched them idea after idea. Then, one day, they said yes. I did a new book with them and have done three more since.

I've had my second chances, and for them I am grateful. Paris has had her second chances and, on this beautiful summer day, appears grateful too. Sally, who is in the class I'm teaching at the Paris Writers Workshop, turns to her partner Meredith, who has accompanied her to Paris, and says, "I'm writing my book this time." Meredith smiles and takes her hand. Why shouldn't Sally manage to write her book? She has made the effort to come to Paris, she has someone who loves her, and, like every writer, she has not come close to using up her chances.

# The Great Escape | 27

Maybe you've received a small inheritance from your grandmother. Maybe you've saved your pennies for years. Maybe you've earned a sabbatical. Maybe you intend to live on plastic and reap the whirlwind later. Whatever your exact circumstances, the die is cast. You are going to Paris for six months, for seven months, for eight months, for as long as you're able to last.

You are ready to live your dream. You drop hints about your upcoming writing jag in Paris, letting co-workers know that you may be quitting, inquiring of your best friend if she'll mind watching your tabby, remarking to your landlord that you may be leaving when the lease expires. You haven't purchased your plane ticket yet, you haven't figured everything out, but you are going, and soon, and for sure. Finally you move from hinting to announcing.

You announce that you are going to Paris to write and, lo and behold, everyone tells you that you shouldn't. Some tell you explicitly and others warn you indirectly. Your mother is one of the direct ones. She tells you that your plan is stupid, self-indulgent, childish, dangerous, and inconsiderate. Your father's reaction is guarded, but no less hurtful. He wanted to write, never did, and is nursing a broken heart. He

has always expressed support for you but didn't help pay for college, and now is mute about Paris, only saying, "I wonder."

Your boss is angry with you—because you've been doing the work of two people, he now may have to hire two people to replace you. He makes frog jokes, leaves you clippings about the vast amounts of dog poop on Parisian streets, and takes the time to explain to you the scams Parisian restaurants pull on unsuspecting tourists ("Do you know what they *put* in cassoulet?"). Your best friend has found eleven reasons why she can't mind your cat, the most charming of which is that adding a litter box would undercut her apartment's feng shui. Even your grandfather, who has always been on your side, is skeptical. "Give up your job?" he says. "To write?"

You know better than all of them. But this complete lack of support hurts your feelings and weakens your resolve. Now, instead of dreaming about Paris, you find yourself having bad dreams about your cat. Suddenly too tired at night to turn your dream into reality, you stop sending out e-mail in pursuit of a cheap studio. You stop looking for good flight deals, carry-on luggage, and a photo shop where you can get some extra passport photos. You stop trying.

One day you decide that you have to thrash this out with your mother, whose reaction has been the most disturbing and heartbreaking. You tell her that you are coming over after dinner to talk about Paris. She wants you to come *for* dinner, but you're watching your weight and living on salads. You have a fight on the phone about that—about your poor eating habits, your weight, your looks, and, naturally, about being single—which sets the stage nicely for the evening's discussion.

When you arrive after dinner, there is a whole cake waiting on the kitchen table in your honor. (Your mother knows you won't touch it, but that won't stop her from making a few choice remarks when you refuse a slice.) You wonder what in God's name you are hoping to accomplish in this tense, overheated kitchen. Finally you plunge ahead.

"The book I'm reading says that I can do it on $1,500 a month," you begin, "so, with a plane ticket, that means I only need $10,000 to stay six months. I've got that $10,000 from Grandma, and I'm going."

Your mother throws up her hands. "Grandma would never have left you that money if she knew that you would throw it away on a trip!" she replies. "And what if it really costs $4,000 a month? You're so gullible! You're always putting too much faith in what people say in books."

"I'm going to rent my studio in Paris before I go. If I can get it for $800 a month, I'm set. I can certainly live on $700 a month for food and incidentals. If I can't get a studio for that little, then I won't go. Isn't that sensible?"

"It's still stupid. What if you get sick?"

"Then I'll get well. Look, I'll purchase travel health insurance."

"And you don't know the language. Do you remember how frightened you were in Mexico when we took that trip—"

"I was seven!"

"Whatever. You still seem frightened to me."

"Thanks."

You take this battering for a full hour. Your father says nothing, which is another blow. There are a hundred opportunities to come to your defense, but he takes none. Finally you get up to leave.

"So you're going to Paris?" your mother demands.

"I am."

"Well, don't expect help from us while you're over there. You'll be six thousand miles away."

"Don't worry. I don't expect help from you."

You may find that your support system is comprised of family, friends, and colleagues who are not actually supportive. You keep hoping for a pat on the back, a good word, some useful help, but instead you get complaints and criticism disguised as advice. Will you let them rob you of Paris? Please don't. In their graceless lack of support, your friends and family may allow you to depart without a *bon voyage* party, and the beginning of your Paris writing adventure may end up feeling furtive, not festive. Still, you must go. On the plane to Paris, buy yourself a glass of champagne and toast your resolve and commitment to yourself.

Who will support you as a writer? Perhaps only *you*, I'm afraid. Who will get you to Paris? *You.* You are your own patron, benefactor, wise aunt. You are the one who must plan your great adventures—and make your great escapes. Your departure for Paris may indeed feel more like a jailbreak than the beginning of a writing adventure. Don't be too disheartened; some helping hands may appear further along the way. But if you are to escape to Paris, you must organize the jailbreak yourself.

# Motivated by Croissants | **28**

The first time I came to Paris I was twenty-seven. I had just completed my first novel, a picaresque about soldiers in Korea, in which I awkwardly transposed my marriage onto characters the Korean DMZ had never seen. That novel, on tissue-thin paper that has survived for thirty years, resides in my storeroom awaiting a major revision.

The first few nights in Paris I stayed at a ratty Left Bank one-star hotel that threw in continental breakfast. That breakfast could not have been simpler: strong coffee, nut-brown croissants, and jam and butter. How I loved that breakfast! The coffee was the best I'd ever tasted (and the best I would taste until I traveled to Italy) and those croissants were to die for— so flaky, so buttery. It seems to me that I got two croissants each morning, a blessing that I still thrill to recollect. If I'm nostalgic for anything in life, it is those croissants.

Then there was the Parisian street food: the small pizzas, the size of tea saucers, topped with green olives; the "Tunisian sandwiches," tuna piled high on crusty rolls; the croques messieurs, those melted ham-and-cheese sandwiches, purchased at a shop across from the Jardins du Luxembourg; and the ubiquitous lamb-filled Greek sandwiches, each topped with a pile of fries. And the baguettes!—well, who hasn't altered his life course at least a little so as to get closer to a crusty baguette?

And the roasted potatoes—potatoes mounded beneath rotisserie chickens, basting in the drippings! I'd pass a certain butcher shop on the Rue Saint Antoine, a shop that always seemed full only of butchers, and stop in my tracks. That orgy of roasting smells! I'd order a few hundred grams of those glistening potatoes and a single chicken leg—or maybe two.

But the best thing I ever ate in Paris, I stole. After those first few nights at that Left Bank hotel, I moved into a room in a flat in the 7th arrondissement, the room of a friend who was away studying in Corsica. The flat had two other occupants, a soft-spoken classical musician and an aristocratic playboy. The playboy brought home a new woman every night and seduced her with food, making his date fancy dishes rivaling Julia Child's. Many of those dishes he would have to start on the weekend, as they involved yards of cheesecloth and days of marinating.

He would sup by candlelight and bed his woman, but not before carefully refrigerating the leftovers.

A Writer's Paris

In the middle of the night, I would sneak into the kitchen and sample that evening's meal. The cold boeuf bourguignonne—the wine sauce, the mushrooms, the fork-tender beef (my God!)—eaten while standing at the refrigerator, was so delicious that I stole not a bite, not two bites, not three bites, but a full portion. Fortunately the playboy with the grand *de* in his name was too superior to mention my nibbling.

Buttery croissants, wine-drenched boeuf bourguignonne—why am I mentioning this? Because if I can make you salivate, I've got you. If I can activate your senses, you're mine. A young writer asked Dostoevsky, "What do you think of my story?" Dostoevsky replied, "When your character drops that coin, *we don't hear it*."

---

That master of psychology knew that readers remain uninvolved until they begin to smell, see, hear, taste … and feel. If you can communicate the ice cream sundaes of your childhood, the fried chicken at weird Aunt Ruthie's, or the croissants of Paris, I am yours. I will read you.

# Running Off | **29**

As a writer, you are built to explore. You were born to run off to the sea, to visit the world's great cities, to investigate the hidden corners of unfamiliar cultures. Therefore, one day, you'll wake up in your Paris bed and cry, "My God, Rome is only an overnight train ride away!" Maybe Berlin will call to you, or Corfu, or Madrid. Your concerns about your budget and your resolve to stay put in Paris will fly right out the window.

That's as it should be. No writer should refuse every siren's call. If you did, how would you have gotten to Paris in the first place? Go to Prague. Go to Oslo. If a wild urge for a new place overcomes you, pack your bags and take off. Brussels is a mere two hours away; London three; Zurich seven; Barcelona eight. Aren't you involuntarily packing already?

During my first stay in Paris I woke up one morning and heard myself murmur *Budapest*. For the next two months I found myself living in a boardinghouse in Pest, on the north side of the Danube. For two dollars you could get a groaning plate of caviar, chopped onions, hard-boiled eggs, and toast points at the café around the corner. I lived on sour cherries and salami in my room and cheap caviar feasts out. I played chess with chess sharks at a high-ceilinged café

**Train Travel Time to Major Cities From Paris**
Brussels, 2 hours
London, 3 hours
Amsterdam, 4 hours
Geneva, 4 hours
Zurich, 6 hours
Nice, 6 hours
Frankfort, 8 hours
Barcelona, 9 hours
Munich, 10 hours
Berlin, 11 hours
Venice, 12 hours
Florence, 13 hours
Madrid, 14 hours
Vienna, 14 hours
Prague, 15 hours
Rome, 15 hours
Copenhagen, 15 hours
Budapest, 18 hours
Krakow, 23 hours

near the river and always lost—though only nickels and dimes. I also scared Woody Allen, in Hungary filming *Love and Death*, by accosting him outside the Buda cathedral.

Run off. Why not? I'm preaching discipline, routine, and an austere writing stint in Paris, but it would be truly horrible not to include the occasional mad trip to Bucharest. Isn't the hunger for herring on a kaiser roll almost as noteworthy as the desire to write your *Iliad*? Run off! If the aroma of broiling wurst is in your

nostrils, if the blue walls of your studio plant Crete in your brain, if strolls along the Canal Saint Martin do not satisfy your need to see Venice, *bon voyage*!

Just don't run away.

Running off is one thing. Running away is another. There are much better stress management tools than fleeing to Florence. Copenhagen is not an anxiety cure. When you wake up and whisper *Amsterdam*, decide if Amsterdam is calling to you or if you are bailing out of your novel. Stare at the wild face in the mirror and inquire, *What's up?* Running off to Lisbon or to Prague is a perfectly fine answer, but only to the right question.

Running away is always a temptation. Every day you may face eleven or thirty-six horrible moments when your screenplay stalls, when your brain wilts, when your energy flags, when your novel feels dead as a doornail. You absentmindedly open a drawer and there, staring you in the face, is the faded manuscript of a novel even duller than your current opus. You scream; you slam the drawer shut; and then you're supposed to return to the computer? How attractive Bucharest looks!

I have run off and I have run away, and I know how hard it is to tell the difference. One clue is how much you've written recently. The more you've written, the less likely it is that you're skipping town to avoid your writing. Still, every day you may be tempted to run away. Every day you may itch for something easier, something different, something to take your mind off the fact that the ending for your story just isn't com-ing. Get ready!

You will certainly wake up one morning in your Paris studio whispering the name of some foreign place or other. Try to run for the right reasons—and make sure you write as soon as you arrive at your des-tination. That's the ticket! Then it won't matter all that much whether you have run off or run away. By picking up your pen and resuming the thread of your novel, you will have earned your adventure. Write beside the bear pits in Bern. Write in a taverna, a Viennese pastry shop, among the cod at the Bergen fish market. Write anywhere—but write.

# With Your Daughter on the Rue de Rivoli | 30

A writer who is also a parent has double leadership duties and can fulfill them both on an excellent sojourn in Paris. If you have your doubts about coming to Paris to write because you have a child, come anyway and make sure to bring her too. Come during the summer, when she is off from school and the weather is warm, and stay for a month. You will both relish Paris and benefit from the experience. Just so long as you adamantly maintain the intention to write, you will write up a storm—even though you have some company.

First, you'll want to peruse the available information on seeing Paris with your children. You'll learn about the Ferris wheel in the Tuileries garden; the Jardin d'Acclimatation in the Bois de Boulogne, touted as the best children's park in Paris; the Parc Astérix, a park themed around the legendary comic-book hero Astérix the Gaul; and of

---

course Disneyland Paris. You'll be told that children like the Bateaux-Mouches that ply the Seine and the interactive Science and Industry Museum (Cité des Sciences et de l'Industrie) at Parc de la Villette, but that they like the Louvre considerably less. That is all sound advice. But it is the two of you together, laughing at a café table, that each of you will remember most vividly. For that you need no preparation except of the following sort.

You do need to prepare your child for your periods of writing. You will want to say something like "Darling, we will have so much fun! But for four or five hours each day I must write. We'll spend an hour in this park or that park and I'll write and you'll chase the pigeons or play on the swings. We'll spend an hour in a café and I'll write and you'll draw or bead. We'll spend an hour in a bookstore and I'll write and you'll read. During those times you may certainly speak to me, but my answers may seem quite strange, as I'll be in Seville with my characters. Does that sound good?"

As soon as you get to Paris with your child, head directly to the Red Wheelbarrow bookstore, located in the Marais at 22 Rue Saint Paul. Pick up your summer reading and make sure to chat with Penelope—Penelope Fletcher Le Masson, the bookstore's Canadian co-proprietor. Penelope is married to Jobic, a French jazz musician, with whom she has had several little ones. Penelope knows Paris and will orient the two of you.

I tell Penelope that I'm writing this book and in two minutes flat she has told me about FUSAC; the American Church; university housing in the 14th arrondissement; family apartments in the 12th; what to do if you speak French; what to do if you don't. Out of gratitude I rush around the corner and buy her an almond tart. She and her bookstore are the sort of resource that will make bringing your child to Paris a pleasure and not a burden. There will be bookstore events for the two of you to attend all through the summer, writers to rub elbows with,

The Children's Red Wheelbarrow bookstore is at 13 Rue Charles V.

and Penelope's hand-selected books for your
summer reading.

I envy you your time with your child! Sunbathe by
the faux beach along the Seine. Walk hand-in-hand
with her on the Rue de Rivoli as you head toward the
Ferris wheel in the Tuileries. Ride the outside escalator
up and down the Centre Pompidou—it has some of
the best views of the roofs of Paris. Sip hot chocolate
together beside the Stravinsky pool. Shop for sou-
venirs. Take a day trip to Giverny or Versailles. Stroll;
stop to write; stop to laugh. What could be better?

I've spent time in Paris alone, time with my wife,
time with one daughter, and time with both my
daughters. My wife and I spent one rainy winter in a
dingy Left Bank hotel. My daughter Kira and I spent
one broiling summer in a small Marais studio. These
good times made for even better memories. By all
means take your child to Paris! Take your husband,
too, and maybe your mother and your three sisters.
Coming to Paris as a lone-wolf artist is not the only
option. Share Paris with a loved one, and do the
bohemian thing family-style.

# Maya and Lemonade

**31**

Say that you're a painter who can't afford to buy expensive pigments. Grudgingly you settle for cheap ones. Then what happens? If you are to stay mentally balanced, you must rationalize. You might reframe the matter as a test of your artistic abilities or as an opportunity for heroism. You might say *These cheap pigments have certain virtues which I intend to understand*. You might say *This will make me strong*. Whatever precise rationalization you use, your goal is to create the adaptive illusion that you are doing just fine.

Consider Van Gogh. Among his many problems was this exact one, the cost of pigments. He couldn't afford the pigments he wanted and turned the lemons of poverty into lemonade by adding the sugar of precedent. He wrote to his brother Theo, who paid for his supplies, "In case you should be a bit hard up, I could manage perfectly without the expensive blues and the carmine. One tube of Prussian blue yields as much as six of ultramarine or cobalt and

costs six times less. Delacroix swore by that vulgar blue and used it often." This is a prayer to Maya, the Hindu goddess whose name translates as *illusion*.

Maya is a necessary god. We must maintain illusions. We must maintain the illusion that what we create matters and that we are not pointless, discardable energy packets but creatures every bit as valuable as our best sentences seduce us into believing that we are. We must create these adaptive illusions and then believe them, even though we know that we ourselves have created them. If you want to know why Existentialists call life absurd, this is why.

I once made this point in a book I was writing, and my editor wrote me a caustic e-mail. "Is this the solution you're proposing? That we maintain adaptive illusions even though we can see right through them? That's not very helpful!" Unfortunately, there's isn't a better answer available. We have become too smart not to know that our cherished beliefs are illusory. Now we must grow into this terrible knowledge and learn how to live in a world that has meaning only if and when we contrive that meaning. This is not an easy job, but at least we, as writers, have the rhetorical skills to create the best-sounding illusions.

Every honest, intelligent person will see through her adaptive illusions often enough. That isn't the main problem. Suddenly writing poetry or stage plays may seem meaningless and ridiculous to you. All right. That realization isn't the danger. The danger is that you will forget that you must maintain your illusions by force of will and that this moment must be met with a hearty *Of course! I always knew that about poetry! Nothing new here!* You must quickly argue yourself back into the belief that poetry matters—at least to you—or face a meaning crisis in proportions you do not want to contemplate.

When you are struck by the thought *My novel serves no ultimate purpose*, you must train yourself to reply *Yes, of course, but I endow it with purpose enough!* There will be moments in Paris when you see that you are not a novelist at the top of her game, but a beginner plodding along on an ugly first draft. Do not let that thought linger uncontested for longer than an instant. Say *A first novel is part of my journey*. Say *I am sure I will be able to salvage the good bits*. Make some kind of lemonade. Otherwise despair will overcome you.

Learning how to chat convincingly with yourself about your meaning-making obligations is the largest part of your education as a creative person. Nobody comes to the table prepared for these conversations or knowledgeable about their subtleties. We learn by living and by periodically losing meaning. Some of us come to the brink of suicide; most of us regularly despair; all of us know the smell of meaninglessness. Honor Maya by darning the rents in the fabric of meaning that is yours to weave.

# If Not Paris, If Not a Year | **32**

If getting away for an extended period of time is out of the question, here's a different plan. Every six months, take a one-week writing jaunt instead. These one-week excursions will serve, just as a year in Paris would, as pillars upon which to build your writing life. These working holidays will be sacred breaks from secular life, the times you set aside for dreaming and intense writing, for strolling and round-the-clock creativity. Maybe they will include some sights, a few choice meals, and a side trip or two, but all of that will be secondary. Their primary purpose will be to reconnect you to your writing dreams and your writing reality.

Space your writing jaunts symmetrically and plan for annual winter and summer sprees. Since Paris can be unpleasantly gloomy in winter, save Paris for summer. In the

winter you might go to Seville instead— which, in January, has two days of sun for each day of rain. Or you might try Hawaii or the Bahamas. (Can you write in paradise? Yes, if your intention is to write. Gauguin managed to paint in Tahiti, after all. Maybe you'll find yourself writing under a beach umbrella rather than in a café, but what sort of problem is that?)

Or you might try a cabin in a snowy place and venture to Maine or Idaho. This is your most dangerous option, as by committing to the isolation of a snow-bound cabin you'll be setting yourself up to do nothing but write—a setup fraught with pressure and expectation. You'll have angels and devils dancing in the flames of your wood fire, unbroken silence, and the splendid or painful firings of your own brain. You could write a whole play in a week, or go insane. Interesting choices!

You have many options, many ways to construct your writing vacations. The main question is: Will you give it a shot? Will you incorporate two or three annual writing stints into your writing life? Most writers won't. They have no trouble seeing themselves attending a poetry workshop in San Miguel de Allende or traveling to Molokai for a spiritual retreat or engaging in cultural travel in Provence. Orchestrating completely self-designed, self-motivated, and self-regulated writing expeditions, however, feels out of the question. The same difficulties that prevent them from writing six days a week at home stop them from planning and executing these precious writing vacations.

There is no end. There is no beginning. There is only the infinite passion of life.
—Federico Fellini

What typically happens? A writer skips his vacation, arguing that he can't take time off. Or he squanders his week, choosing a locale and a theme that prove boring by the end of the second day. Or, having planned nothing and finding his vacation upon him, he sits at home in the dark, waiting for his day job to resume. Or he convinces himself that studying with a French chef or learning boat-building in Oslo is every bit as creative as writing. Over time his vacations become a sore point, something that he would rather not think about—something that, as odd as it sounds,

he almost wishes didn't exist. The idea of spending a week in an evocative locale connected and committed to his writing never quite bobs into consciousness— or, if it does, is quickly submerged again.

I'm sure that you'd like to prove yourself a constant writer, someone who writes at home most days of the week and goes to a faraway place a few times each year to write some more. Naples, Mazatlán, Aspen, Berlin— the world is your writing oyster. Reframe your annual vacations as pillars of your writing life. Include Paris— or not. Paris is not everyone's cup of tea and it may not be yours. Where would *you* like to go? Choose your own sacred sites, those special places where you're bound to write up a storm.

A Writer's Paris

# Fearing Paris | **33**

Maybe you fear coming to Paris to write. But is it really Paris that you fear? My hunch is that it isn't. I doubt that you fear not knowing the language, ending up in a closet-size studio, or subjecting yourself to a supercilious shrug or two. I bet that the thought of managing your affairs from an Internet café or buying a foreign shampoo doesn't seem all that daunting. My hunch is that what you fear, if you fear anything, is bringing into consciousness a trunk full of painful thoughts about your writing past, present, and future.

I'm convinced that you could visit Paris without a moment's hesitation if writing weren't on the agenda. An eating trip to Paris, a museum jaunt, a shopping spree—such adventures wouldn't activate your anxieties in the slightest. The real problem is your relationship to your writing. You fear opening up a can of worms. If you entertained the idea of writing in Paris, you would raise the ghosts of buried short stories, quarter-written novels, poems with their last lines missing. Better all that stay dead and buried!

For many people, the idea of writing in Paris is tied up with feelings of pain and disappointment. It is bound up with too many failed attempts to get up early and write, too many missed appointments to

sneak in five hundred words after a wearying day at the office. It is associated with a hundred ruined plans and a thousand broken promises. Paris, a self-doubting writer supposes, is a place reserved for *real* writers, ones who regularly write and publish. How can they consider themselves one of those, given their lack of output, their lack of completed pieces, their lack of success? Writing in Paris, they conclude, is a gift they haven't earned and don't deserve.

It isn't that they fear Paris. It is that they are too down on themselves. They can picture themselves visiting the Louvre or strolling in the Tuileries; they just can't picture themselves actually writing. They believe they know themselves too well to paint a mental picture of Paris that includes an actual pad, an actual pen, and the actual activity of writing. They are truthful enough that they don't want to feed themselves that fib—that they would write in Paris when they haven't written at home for months. However, by being truthful in this fashion they promote a different lie: That they are barren and hopeless.

They are courageous enough not to indulge themselves in what is known as the "geographic fallacy"—the

idea that alcoholics (for instance) would miraculously stop drinking if only they moved to Boise or Berlin. These honest nonwriting writers announce, "I'm not writing here in Pittsburgh, and therefore I won't write in Paris either. Why lie about it?" But doesn't an answer suggest itself?

The cure for this fear is simply to begin writing where you are. Every writing day in Pittsburgh is a day earned toward Paris. Every week is a week. Every month is a month. If you write for a full year at your own desk in your own bedroom, you would earn the right to spend a year writing in Paris. By writing in Pittsburgh, you would join local heroes everywhere who write where they find themselves. By writing in Pittsburgh, you would purchase Paris on the layaway plan.

My deplorable mania for analysis exhausts me. I doubt everything, even my doubt.
　　—Gustave Flaubert

It takes real resilience to come back from so many lost writing days, so many half-baked manuscripts, so many market-place blows, so many broken promises. Sometimes just a single blow—a curt rejection, an unrealized manuscript—can trau-matize you and reduce your motivation to zero. Someone who doesn't write can smile at such hyperbole, at the way we claim that a rejection letter can rise to the level of trauma. But we know. We have invested so much in our writing—maybe everything—that when we fail at our writing or the marketplace slaps our writing away there is no other word to use but *traumatic*.

If you fear that you are unequal to the writing life and if, nevertheless, you mean to give yourself the gift of Paris, you will need to forgive yourself for your past failures and draw on the well of courage that you indubitably possess. If you want Paris but a terrible fear courses through you when you bring the subject up to yourself, these are the answers: forgiveness and courage. You must believe that good writing awaits you; and then you must make your arrangements.

# Au Revoir to the Place des Vosges | **34**

I hope that you'll go to Paris and write. Right now, though, you need to write precisely where you are, with dirty dishes in the sink, bills piled high by the phone, and snow falling not on cedar, but on your dilapidated car. It is wishful thinking to believe that you will write somewhere else when you haven't been writing where you live—a fiction that is easy to love because it promises effortless masterpieces and jasmine-scented evenings. Don't succumb. Paris is a beautiful dream and a doable reality, but not an excuse for not writing at home.

As you sit in your apartment, your task is to tackle your novel or your short story and then tackle the world of book publishers or quarterlies. To help buoy your spirits as you work away, access the Paris already inside of you. There is a Paris-of-the-mind that resides in each of us, a Paris of Hemingway and Camille Claudel, of Gertrude Stein and Romaine Brooks, her salon rival. There is a Paris-of-the-mind made up of a thousand stories, a million images communicated in books and movies. It is available to you right now.

As has been said about God, if Paris did not exist we would have had to invent her, so profound is our attraction to what she represents. We need Henry

Miller and Anaïs Nin entwined, we need the student protests of 1968, we need Abelard castrated in Notre Dame as retribution for his love of Héloïse. We need the chestnut trees, the cafés, the bookstalls, the out-looks on the Seine. We need them and, luckily, we have them, tucked away in a corner of consciousness, ready to be rolled out with or without a glass of wine.

You don't have to hang Toulouse Lautrec posters on your wall or place Gauguin coasters on your coffee table to taste Paris. Just close your eyes. You can be in the Place des Vosges, sitting and writing, whenever you like. You can be walking the boulevards of Saint Germain des Prés beside Jean-Paul Sartre and Simone de Beauvoir. It will help if you've been to the real Paris, but that hardly matters. Paris is part of our shared vocabulary, alive in the hearts and minds of artists everywhere. Can't you picture Paris right now?

But by all means add some icons to your environment. A postcard, a blue vase, a framed photograph, a coaster, café music, this book—use such totems and mementos to keep Paris alive. I keep a postcard in front of me of a scene that might be anywhere in Europe. The sun is rising over a cobblestone street, a leafy tree overhangs four or five empty café tables,

A Writer's Paris

centuries-old buildings with their steeply sloped roofs stand cheek by jowl in the cold morning light. It is a postcard that I gave to one of my daughters and then stole back. Now it faces me as I write.

I have Paris even when I'm not there. But when I'm there, it's hard to leave her. Just as it's the first place I visit when I arrive, the Place des Vosges is where I take my leave. I give it a whole afternoon. I sit on the western side of the park, musing about Georges Simenon and Josephine Baker, who consummated their affair a hundred yards away; or perhaps about a certain Camus essay, penned the night of Paris's liberation,

in which joy and thanks mingle with pessimism and sorrow. And I do a little writing.

Dusk falls. The park's guard, looking every bit the toy soldier, cries out that the Place des Vosges is closing. Lovers, asleep on their blankets, rouse themselves; the last tourists shut their guidebooks. In the morning I'm off to the Gallieni bus station to catch the bus for London. I'm sure I'll arrive early enough to do some writing and watch some dramas unfold. Maybe someone won't be allowed to board our bus. Would I mind if it were me?

I don't know if it's intelligence that makes the writer—or heart, or hard work, or an existential feel, or that thing called talent. I don't know if each of a billion people could write an excellent novel, or if only a thousand can. I don't know if you leave the womb already a writer, or if writing is a decision you make as you look around for a path you can love. What I do know is that, if you have read this book to the end, you belong to our family. Since our family vacations in Paris, I'm sure our paths will cross in the Place des Vosges. You may be lost in thought and not notice me, but not to worry. I'll be lost in thought, too.

# A Planning Checklist  | **A1**

The following is a modest checklist to help you keep track of your Paris preparations. If you're flying off for a week, you can leave almost on the spur of the moment. If you're going for longer than that, do some real planning.

### Chat and Negotiate

Unless you are entirely unencumbered, financially set, and you don't need the services of others to watch your cat, handle your mail, and so on, you will need to chat—and negotiate—with the people you leave behind. These discussions ought to be serious, sit-down conversations about duties and responsibilities—yours and theirs—that culminate in clear agreements. You might want to begin a full year in advance, especially if you need to prepare people emotionally for your departure.

### Articulate Your Goals

Get a small notebook and begin to articulate your goals for your time in Paris. Your goals might be abstract (for instance to write deeply and to visit the environs of Paris) or specific (to write three hundred pages in three months and to visit Giverny, Versailles,

and Fontainebleau). Whether abstract or specific, they should be moved from your subconscious to paper so that you can appraise them and edit them as necessary.

**Calculate Costs**

Prepare a real budget and make it as accurate as you can. You may find it daunting and demoralizing to see concrete figures based on a real dollar-to-euro exchange rate, and you may realize that you will need more money than you had supposed or imagined. But this exercise is also an opportunity to create a lean Paris lifestyle and prune items that you can do without from your budget. Of course, by far your largest expense will be your housing, which means ...

**Look Into Housing**

Start to think about your housing needs. Will you opt for the cheapest, smallest, highest-up studio in a not-excellent neighborhood, or are you pining for a decent place in the Marais or across from the Jardins du Luxembourg? Order your subscription to *FUSAC* or visit it online, hunt the Internet for Parisian rental information, make Parisian friends by joining chat groups, study the guidebooks, and educate yourself about Parisian short-term housing. (See "The Doable Dream" on Pages 91-97.) You may decide to select your place once you get to Paris and not before; but even so, the more information you gather, the more prepared you'll be on arrival.

## Raise the Money

Few Americans save, so you will have to prove the exception if your plan is to pay for your Paris trip with savings. If it takes you three years to save enough, then it takes you three years. During that time you can write up a storm and earn Paris on two levels—by accruing both funds and karma. You might also raise the money by approaching your parents or grandparents, or by trying to cadge the odd grant or scholarship. (Think three times before putting your sojourn on plastic.) If your plan is to live by working, research work options like freelance writing, ghostwriting, travel writing, and other revenue streams. Read the working-in-Paris guides and Internet information, hone the skills that you're likely to need (for instance, French), make contacts from afar, and, if you can, secure your job before you go.

### Create a Timeline

Create a timeline that includes purchasing your ticket, getting your passport, subletting your apartment, storing your belongings, practicing your Paris routine, and so on. The list you create of pending tasks is likely to be a very long one, which is daunting—but the list will also ground your sojourn in reality. The less real your trip feels, the more likely you'll be to let it slide into the ever-receding future. Make a list as long as your arm of the tasks confronting you, and bravely transfer those tasks onto your timeline.

### Prepare Your Writing and Your Writing Business

What writing project will you work on while in Paris? If you're bringing a current project along, whip it into workable shape. If you intend to start a new project in Paris, decide whether you'll begin writing it at home and arrive with preliminary notes or whether you'll wait until you get to Paris before beginning. Give this matter real thought, as there may be excellent reasons for bringing your current troublesome manuscript and equally excellent reasons for putting it aside and starting on something fresh.

At the same time, create a plan to manage your writing business. Will you be sending out your short stories while you write in Paris? If so, how will you handle that? Can a friend be enlisted to circulate manuscripts? Certainly you'll want a Web-based e-mail address—and probably a cell phone with international service (not all U.S. cell phones work in Europe) and a laptop computer with wireless capability.

### Practice Your Paris Routine

In the weeks before you leave, use a couple of consecutive Sundays to practice your Paris routine. Get up early, pack your writing supplies, find a place to write—the town square, the mall, the junior college, the local deli—and write. Write for two hours, stroll a bit, find a second writing venue—a fast-food joint, a doughnut shop, a Starbucks—and write some more. Stroll again, locate a third writing spot—the library, the Christian Science Reading Room—and write again. When you get home, assess the day. Notice how much writing you got done, how righteous you feel—and how exhausted.

## Get Set and Go

Sleepless nights. Your adrenaline is pumping. Paris is approaching. Your cat has been boarded. Your best friend has pledged to e-mail you daily. You still have thirty things left to do, but your list is down from two hundred. You've decided to begin a new novel when you get to Paris, and scenes from that novel are beginning to flood your consciousness. Are you ready? Not really. But off you go!

# Where to Write or Read

If a number in parentheses is provided, it refers back to the essay where the location was mentioned.

### Anglophone Bookstores

Red Wheelbarrow (30)
22 rue Saint Paul (Marais)
www.theredwheelbarrow.com
Take the Métro to St. Paul. The children's store is at 13 rue Charles V.

Shakespeare & Company (25)
37 rue de la Bûcherie (Latin Quarter)
www.shakespeareco.org
Just across from Notre Dame. Take the Métro to St. Michel.

Village Voice Bookshop (23)
6 rue Princesse (Saint Germain-des-Prés)
www.villagevoicebookshop.com
Take Métro to Saint Germain-des-Prés.

### A Few Cafés

Au Chien Qui Fume (The Dog Who Smokes)
33 rue du Pont-Neuf (Les Halles)
www.au-chien-qui-fume.com
Open until 2 a.m. Take the Métro to Les Halles.

Les Deux Magots (07)
6 Place Saint Germain des Prés
www.lesdeuxmagots.fr
Filled with tourists due its association with former
frequenters, Hemingway and Sartre. Take the Métro to Saint
Germain-des-Prés. Try Le Café de Flore next door if Les Deux
Magots feels too touristy.

Le Procope (07)
13 rue de l'Ancienne Comédie (Latin Quarter)
www.procope.com
Oldest restaurant in Paris and first café. Its regulars included
Voltaire, Balzac, Hugo, and Zola. Take the Métro to Odéon.

## Day Trips

Monet's Giverny (07)
http://giverny.org
Giverny by train (45 minutes): Start at Saint-Lazare station and take
the train to Vernon (about 25 Euro). Closed during winter months.

Château de Chantilly (08)
www.chateaudechantilly.com
Chantilly by train (30 minutes): Start at Gare du Nord and take the
train to Chantilly-Gouvieux (about 5-10 Euro).

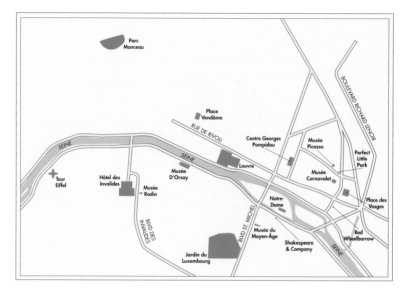

Fontainebleau (08)

www.musee-chateau-fontainebleau.fr

Home of all French sovereigns since the Middle Ages.

Fontainebleau by train (40 minutes): Start at Gare de Lyon and

take the train to Fontainebleau-Avon (about 10 Euro).

Château de Versailles (25)

www.chateauversailles.fr

Versailles by train (30 minutes): Take the RER-C train starting from

Gare d'Austerlitz or any other RER stop (about 5 Euro round-trip).

Get off at Versailles Rive Gauche.

## Selected Museums

L'Espace Dalie (Salvador Dali Museum) (25)

11 rue Poulbot, Place du Tertre (Montmartre)

www.daliparis.com

Take the Métro to Anvers or Abbesses.


Musée d'Art Américain (08)

www.maag.org

At Giverny—see previous listing.


Musée Carnavalet (08)

23 rue de Sévigné

www.paris.fr/musees/musee_carnavalet

Learn the history of Paris. Closed Mondays. Take Métro to Saint-Paul or Chemin Vert.


Musée du Louvre (25)

www.louvre.fr

The Mona Lisa museum. Not hard to find, just use the Métro stop named after it. Closed Tuesdays.


Musée de la Musique (25)

221 Avenue Jean Jaurès

www.cite-musique.fr

Concerts and museum. Take Métro to Porte de Pantin.

Musée National des Arts Asiatiques (Guimet)

6 place d'Iéna

www.museeguimet.fr

Take Métro to Iéna. Delightful Asian art collection, complete with Buddhas. Closed Tuesdays.

Centre Pompidou (24)

1 rue Beaubourg

www.cnac-gp.fr

Take Métro to Chatelete/Les Halles. Modern and contemporary art collection housed in an archictecturally thrilling space. Open late. Closed Tuesdays.

Musée National du Moyen Age (02)

(Musée de Cluny)

6 place Paul Painlevé

www.musee-moyenage.fr

National museum of the Middle Ages, which includes the ancient architecture of the Gallo-Roman baths. Take Métro to Métro Cluny-La Sorbonne. Closed Tuesdays.

Musée d'Orsay (04)

62 rue de Lille

www.musee-orsay.fr

Take the Métro to Solférino. Enter on the side of the river Seine if you don't have a reserved ticket. Use rue de Lille if you do. Closed Mondays.

Musée Rodin (14)

77 rue de Varenne (near Napoleon's Tomb)

www.musee-rodin.fr

Take the Métro to Varenne. Closed Mondays.

Musée du Vieux Montmartre (25)

12 rue Cortot

Dedicated to the history of Montmartre. Take Métro to Lamarck-Caulaincourt or Abbesses. Closed Mondays.

Musée Picasso

5 rue de Thorigny

In Marais, near Place des Vosges. Take Métro to St. Paul or Chemin Vert. Closed Tuesdays.

## Parks

Bois de Boulogne (02)

Enormous park on western edge of Paris. Favorite destination of

Parisian walkers, bicyclists, and horse riders. Take the Métro to
Porte Dauphine.

Bois de Vincennes (02)
www.boisdevincennes.com
Does for the east side of Paris what Boulogne does for the west.
Take the Métro to Porte Dorée.

Jardin d'Acclimatation (in Bois de Boulogne) (30)
www.jardindacclimatation.fr
It'll cost you a couple Euro to get in. Take the Métro to Les Sablons.

Jardin du Luxembourg (25)
In the Latin Quarter and near the Sorbonne. Great if you have kids
(lots of play areas and activities). Take the Métro to Odéon.

Jardin des Plantes (15)
The main botanical garden in France, which contains the
oldest tree in Paris. Also offers a zoo and other attractions for adults
and children alike. Plan a picnic lunch by stopping at the nearby
food market on rue Mouffetard. Take the Métro to Gare d'Austerlitz.

Jardin Saint Gilles Grand Veneur (15)
A quiet spot in Marais at rue Villehardouin. Take Métro to Chemin Vert.

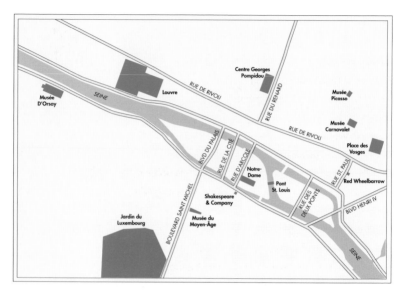

Jardin des Tuileries

You'll find a merry-go-round, donkey rides, and small boats for
hire. Take the Métro to Palais Royal.

Parc des Buttes Chaumont (15)

Different from most Parisian parks—more American style. Take the
Métro to Buttes-Chaumont.

Parc Monceau (15)

Full of architectural follies. Take the Métro to Monceau.

Parc Montsouris (02)

Borders Cité Universitaire (housing for students). Take the Métro to Porte d'Orléans or Cité Universitaire.

Parc de la Villette (15)

www.villette.com/us/mainprog.htm

More than just a green space, this area offers leisure activities, expositions, shows and debates. Take Métro to Porte de Pantin.

## Markets

Boulevard Richard-Lenoir (03)

Largest market in Paris, every Thursday and Sunday, between Place de la Bastille and rue St. Sabin, opening at 7 a.m. to 2:30 p.m. Thursdays and 3 p.m. Sundays. Take Métro to Bastille.

Rue Montorgueil

Near the Louvre and Pompidou. Closed Mondays. Take the Métro to Etienne Marcel.

Rue Mouffetard

Get yourself a picnic lunch here before relaxing in the Luxembourg Garden. Closed Mondays. Take the Métro to Cardinal Lemoine.

Rue Cler

Near the Eiffel Tower. No traffic on this street makes the market a pleasure to shop. Closed Mondays. Take the Métro to Ecole Militaire.

## For Children and Families

Cité des Sciences et de l'Industrie (30)
www.cite-sciences.fr
Science and industry museum. Take the Métro to Porte de la Villette. Closed Mondays.

Parc Astérix (30)
www.parcasterix.com
Amusement park, about 30-35 Euro per person for one day. Take the Métro/RER B3 line, from Châtelet or Gare du Nord stations. Get off at Roissy-Charles-de-Gaulle 1 station.

Disneyland Paris (30)
www.disneylandparis.com
Knock yourself out.

Many of the parks are wonderful as well—see previous listings.

# Resources for Planning Your Trip | **A3**

Nearly all of the housing resources and Paris guidebooks were mentioned in Essay 16, "The Doable Dream."

### Web Sites

Paris Pages
www.paris.org
This site has a search function for English-language info about various Paris attractions, neighborhoods, housing, etc.

EscapeArtist.com
www.escapeartist.com
Geared toward expatriates.

Parler Paris
www.parlerparis.com
Subscribe to their free newsletter.

### Housing References

Allo Logement Temporaire
www.allo-logement-temporaire.asso.fr
They'll hunt for your housing for a fee.

American Church
www.acparis.org
65 Quai d'Orsay
Interdenominational fellowship; many services for expatriate
English-speaking community, including an "Ad Board"
(not available on Web site). Take the Métro to Invalides.

*De Particulier à Particulier*
www.pap.fr
Print publication with online companion. Only the site will give
you English listings.

*FUSAC* (France USA Contacts)
www.fusac.fr
Free magazine distributed in Paris for English-speaking community.
Online version available.

*Paris Voice*
www.parisvoice.com
In English, similar to *FUSAC*.

## Guidebooks

*Hello France!: Best Budget Hotels in France* by Margo Classe.
www.helloeurope.com

*Writers Insider Guide to Paris* by Elizabeth Reichert.
E-book available through www.parlerparis.com

*Around and About Paris* by Thirza Vallois.

Once you're in Paris, you'll want to pick up
entertainment listings—try either *L'officiel des Spectacles* or
*Pariscope* (both in French, but decipherable with some help).

## Nonfiction and Memoir

Nin, Anaïs. *The Diary of Anaïs Nin.*
Rodriguez-Hunter, Suzanne. *Found Meals of the Lost Generation:
Recipes and Anecdotes From 1920s Paris.*
Rosenblum, Mort. *The Secret Life of the Seine.*

## Fiction

Baldwin, James. *Giovanni's Room.*
Black, Cara. *Murder in the Marais.*
Black, Cara. *Murder in the Sentier.*
Camus, Albert. *Exile and the Kingdom.*
Camus, Albert. *The First Man.*
Gordon, Karen. *Paris Out of Hand.*
Simenon, Georges. Inspector Maigret mysteries and psychological
novels (*Monsieur Monde Vanishes, Sunday, November*).

## About the Author

Eric Maisel is the author of more than twenty-five works of fiction and nonfiction. His nonfiction titles include *Coaching the Artist Within*, *Fearless Creating*, *The Van Gogh Blues*, *The Creativity Book*, and *The Performance Anxiety Workbook*. A columnist for *Art Calendar* magazine and a regular contributor to *Artist's Sketchbook*, *Writer's Digest*, and *The Writer* magazines, Maisel is a San Francisco–based creativity coach and coach trainer who presents keynote addresses and workshops nationally and internationally.

Visit www.ericmaisel.com to learn more, or write the author at ericmaisel@hotmail.com.